The Gospel in Soul & State:

Life, Leadership, and Politics from a Biblical Perspective

Kahlib J. Fischer, PhD
Liberty University

Scripture quotations are from the ESV® Bible (The Holy Bible, English Standard Version®), copyright © 2001 by Crossway, a publishing ministry of Good News Publishers. Used by permission. All rights reserved. The ESV text may not be quoted in any publication made available to the public by a Creative Commons license. The ESV may not be translated into any other language.

Cover image © Shutterstock, Inc.

www.kendallhunt.com
Send all inquiries to:
4050 Westmark Drive
Dubuque, IA 52004-1840

Copyright © 2023 by Kahlib Fischer

ISBN 979-8-7657-4277-8

Kendall Hunt Publishing Company has the exclusive rights to reproduce this work, to prepare derivative works from this work, to publicly distribute this work, to publicly perform this work and to publicly display this work.

All rights reserved. No part of this publication may be reproduced, stored in a retrieval system, or transmitted, in any form or by any means, electronic, mechanical, photocopying, recording, or otherwise, without the prior written permission of the copyright owner.

Published in the United States of America

TABLE OF CONTENTS

Preface vii
Introduction ix

PART I 1

Chapter 1 Heart of Hearts: The Realm of the Intrapersonal 3
    Introduction 3
    Who We Were: Rebels, Orphans, and Slaves 3
    Who We Are: Vulnerability and Intimacy in Christ 7
        Propitiation 7
        Justification 8
        Redemption 9
        Reconciliation 9
        Adoption 11
    Illusions of Self-Sufficiency, Addictions, and Dehumanization 11
    Healthy Vulnerability 12
    Christian Perfectionism/Legalism: A Question of Who Gets the Glory 13
    What Are We Saying Yes To? 15

Chapter 2 Covenant and Interpersonal Relationships 17
    Introduction 17
    The Theology of Covenant 18
    Hesed: In Spirit and in Truth 18
    Mutual Empowerment, Appreciation, and Accountability 19
    Empowerment and Collaboration 20
    Wonderful, Beautiful Boundaries 21

God's Family, Your Family 22
    Beautiful Imaginations 22
    Husbands and Wives, Parents and Children 24

Chapter 3 Of Conflicts, Churches, and Covenants 27
  Peace-Breaking, Peace-Faking, and Peace-Making 27
  Some Helpful Tips for Conflict Resolution 29
    We Are Almost Always Part of the Problem 29
    Conflict Stems from Our Beloved, Wonderful Personality Traits 29
    Conflict Is Inevitable 30
    Beware the Dangers of Unmet, Unspoken Expectations.................................. 30
    Conflict Can Be an Opportunity to Grow 31
  Church Life and Conflict.. 31
    Do Not Idolize Church Leadership 32
    Limit Your Involvement: Avoid Gossip and Slander 32
    Perfect Conflict Resolution Will Not Happen This Side of Heaven 33
    Do Not Idolize Your Vision for Ministry 33
    Conflict Resolution Prevents Evil 34
  Conclusion 34

PART II 37

Chapter 4 Interpersonal Dimensions of Organizational Leadership 41
  An Unhappy Personal Note 41
  Leadership Basics 42
    A Working Definition of Leadership 42
    Leadership vs. Management 43
  Between God and Man: Imago Dei 44
    Fearfully and Wonderfully Made—Personal Attributes of Leadership 44
    The Nature of Empowerment 45
    Sin and the Problem of Selfish Empowerment 46
    Servant Leadership and Following Christ 46
    Transformational Leadership and Covenant Keeping 47
    Authentic Leadership and the Cross of Christ 47
  Idols of Leadership 48
    Raging Control or Abdication 48
    The Promotion Fallacy 48

    Avoiding Vision-Killers 49
    Measurement, Management, and Manipulation 49
    The Idolatry of Wanting Results 50
    A Worthy Leadership Goal 50

Chapter 5 Leadership as Applied to Organizational Structure, Processes, and Culture 51
  A Covenantal Emphasis on Organizational Leadership 51
    Hesed 51
    Mutual Accountability 52
    Federalism and Noncentralization 52
  Hesed in the Organizational Context: Culture and Communication 52
    Communication among Leaders and Followers 52
    Building a Shared Vision 53
  Mutual Accountability and Organizational Processes 53
    Decision-Making, Active Dialogue, and Big Picture Thinking 53
    Performance Management 54
  Noncentralization and Organizational Structure 55
    Noncentralization vs. Decentralization 55
    Boundaryless Communication 55
  Thoughts on a Covenantal Culture 55
    Covenant, Empowerment, and Self-Sustaining Culture 55
    Explaining Postmodernism 56
    Covenant and Spirituality in the Workplace 58
  Covenant as an Integrative Paradigm 58

Chapter 6 Personal Foundations of Justice and Society 61
  Introduction 61
  God's Character: Love and Justice, Natural Law, Church and State 65
    Overview 65
    Justice 67
  The Nature of Man: Inalienable Rights and Limited Government 69
    Inalienable Rights 69
    The Multi-Faceted Conundrum of Sin 72
    Historical Developments 73

Chapter 7 Corporate Facets of Justice, Society and Government 77
  The Conundrum of Legislation Morality (or Trying Not To) 77
  The Relationship between God and Man: Covenant and Church-State Relations 78

- The Church and State Must Have Separate Functions 80
- Separation of Church and State Does Not Mean a Separation of the State from Biblical Principles 82
- Historical Evidence 82
- Man and Man: Covenant, Mutual Accountability, Federalism, and Noncentralization 84
  - Review 84
  - A Progression of Covenants: Creation and Redemption 86
  - Historical Roots of the Covenant Idea 88
- Selfless Self-Defense: Resisting Tyranny 89
  - Overview 89
  - Historical Evidence 93

Chapter 8 The Culture Wars: The Battle of Ideas in Public Life 95
- Introduction 95
- Christian Legalism: Statism, Racism, and Chauvinism 96
- Over-reactions to Over-reactions—the Rise of the Modern Man 98
- The Flight to Postmodernism 99
- Marxism: The Abiding Infatuation 100
- Gospel Implications 101
  - Sexual Intimacy and Family Life 102
  - Privilege and Racism 104
- The Impacts of False Gods 106
- The Gospel and Covenant vs. the Isms 107

Chapter 9 Where Angels Fear to Tread—Thoughts on Public Policy 111
- Rebels and the Power of Elites 111
  - Regulations That Favor the Powerful at the Expense of Competition 112
  - Economic Planning That Protects Greed 113
- Orphanhood and Idolizing the State 114
- Slavery: Regulations That Undermine Self-Government 114
- Reformation, Not Revolution; Substance, Not Structuralism 116
- Covenant and Tools for Sound Policy 117

Conclusion 119
References 121
Index 123

PREFACE

This is a book for professionals in the realms of business, government, economics, and the like, so that your heart would not grow cold as you engage in the tasks of your profession, that you would not put your hope in your professional striving, status, and accomplishments, that you would not fail to see the connection between who you are as a human made in God's image and the role you play in the battlefield of politics and business, and that you would not forget that you are a child of God first and foremost, both in need of a Savior, and in receipt of that Savior's love and grace. So, while this book will at times discuss political, economic, organizational, structural, and even philosophical concepts, I pray that the ideas you find here will call you back home into the loving arms of your Father, and keep you there.

But this book is also for someone who may never work in any high level of government, or business, or even be noticed by the upper echelons of society. But maybe you are involved in ministry, either full time or as part of your church life. If this is you, I pray that in reading this book you may be encouraged that by resting in Christ's saving work, and loving others accordingly, and remembering that you are now a child of God, that your actions very much shape and preserve the destiny of your family, your community, and your homeland. Yes, at times this text will focus on more academic jargon, but I hope you will be encouraged to know that in the end, it is not the wisdom of the sages or the technocrats that wins the day, but always God's work in the realm of our heart and souls, and then in the realm of intimacy with others. You are known and loved by God, and your actions in even simple things have long-lasting, far-ranging, and eternal impacts. You are a child of God, or at least can be if you do not yet know Him. Thus, no matter your station in life, living as a royal child of the King ensures that your actions bear the marks of eternal import and impact.

This book is also for the radicals—the Marxists, postmodernists, atheists, and many more. We will not agree on everything, but at the very least, I hope you will take comfort in the fact that this book leaves no quarter for an enculturated, legalistic, dead Christianity—the corpse of which has been the foundation for atrocities such as racism, slavery, chauvinism, nationalism, and imperialism. I hope you will find that in contrast, this book offers an opportunity to look beyond merely structural and secular concerns for the cause of what ails us, to the solution, found in Christ, who resolves all of the worldview necessities of a coherent life—epistemology, axiology, ontology, and teleology. And, I should add, there are many good and heart-broken people who no longer feel comfortable calling themselves Christians or evangelicals because of this very problem—this whitewashed tombstone that is legalistic, perfectionist, reductionist Christianity. If this describes you, hopefully this book will be a balm for your soul.

For the atheist, in particular, let me offer a sympathetic note for you as you move forward in this book: it can be challenging to make sense of what Christians claim to believe. Sure, there are the miraculous interventions of a divine being claimed often in Scripture, most notably in the resurrection of Christ. But this book focuses on a more subtle dimension of the human experience, which is not limited to nor fully existent in the physical realm—the very heart and soul of man. So, when we talk about loving selflessly and caring for others—something that most humans understand and aspire to—whether Christian or not, and perhaps sadly often not—we argue that this is only possible owing to a metaphysical prerequisite that transcends motivations for self-survival, or social-cultural conventions, the time-space continuum, or the combinations of physical forces which in and of themselves cannot create fixed, absolute rules of logic. The Bible describes God as being triune and in perfect fellowship, who then, as the divine *logos*, took on flesh, and walked into time and space and dwelt among us. And yes, while He performed many miracles of healing, storm-calming, and even resurrection, He came to heal our hearts and souls and bring us back into fellowship with our loving Father. I understand that talking about hearts and souls, and pointing to concepts such as personal, individual sentience, aided by the rules of logic to communicate, is the very thing that you as a hard-core empiricist would deny. I do not agree of course, and I will speak to this in ways below, but I am sympathetic to the conundrum this text might present. The difference between the Christian worldview and the atheist-naturalistic view is a gap not easily jumped. But nevertheless, I just wanted to say "hello" and I hope you will keep reading.

And finally, on a personal note, one of the greatest gifts you can give to me as the author of this book is diligent reading undone by introspection and deep thinking. When I was a student, I would often get mad at myself for being distracted by the tangents and musings that inevitably come with reading a book seriously and thoughtfully. Diligent students often feel the pressure of so much reading and homework, so it took me many years to realize that those musings were likely the most important part of the reading (and learning) process. In that vein, I hope this book does the same to you, not because I desire to get you off schedule, but because I am, whole-heartedly, trying to encourage some deep thinking and reflection on your part. Thus, I pray that you will be encouraged to see that in the profound and the practical, in the simple and the complex, and the personal and the philosophical, the Gospel of Jesus Christ and His covenant with us is the great unifier—in matters of soul and state, the "heart of the matter is always a matter of the heart."

▶ Throughout the book whenever this play icon appears, go to https://www.khpcontent.com/ to view a video related to the chapter.

INTRODUCTION

I always struggled to stay awake in class, from high school through college. I always meant well—always tried to shake off the impending doom of sleep, but rarely succeeded. Sometimes it felt like I was getting whiplash as my head jerked up suddenly when I would nod off and then wake up again. And there was also my note-taking that would look like flatlining on a heart monitor every time I nodded off. There were also rumors of drool being involved, which I steadfastly deny. But nevertheless: I only share that to say that I personally cannot imagine how difficult it might be to serve as a soldier and then, in that capacity, have to stay up all night on guard.[1]

But back to the scenario of the poor soldiers on guard: this is the opening example of this book. Imagine guarding a tomb of some revolutionary, a hero of the people, now executed by a powerful emperor. This revolutionary was so dangerous that even after death, guards surround his tomb, for fear that his followers might steal his body and claim some sort of resurrection. Political and religious leaders alike know the dangers that these types of rumors breed: both insurrection and heresy. Sure, the heavy stone laying across the door of the tomb is not going to move itself, but there the guards stand on duty, perhaps trying desperately to stay awake like me in class, in the dark of night, making sure that the stone, in fact, remained in place.

Of course, the most important point here is that thdis is the setting in AD 33 at the tomb of a man named Jesus Christ. He was indeed a hero of the people of Israel—an oppressed people group caught under the heels of the world's most powerful empire. Or at least he was until he made it clear that he was not bringing a military and political uprising. But his claims of divinity and his words of peace and reconciliation with God at the level of heart and soul were so revolutionary that the religious elites of his time were convinced that he had to die. And so, he did die, gruesomely on the cross, as so many other self-proclaimed messiahs of that age did. Along with those, his death should have been just another passing moment of

---

[1] I also share this to draw attention to the fact that I have a very dry sense of humor, which will manifest itself in this book from time to time. It is good to chuckle a bit while trying to parse through a lot of intensely personal and academic concepts.

false hope long lost in the grinding gears of history. And yet, whatever you and I may understand about Christianity, we know that his story and impact have not ended.

Here, then, is one way of making sense of his impact: so much what ails us in this life was present at the resurrection at Christ's tomb. Imagine being the guards sent there to watch the tomb and prevent some sort of shenanigans on the part of supposed religious zealots. Yes, those guards were there by Pilate's command, but Pilate only ordered them there at the urging of the Pharisees. Now Pilate often viewed the Pharisees with contempt and exasperation, but he was in a difficult position, needing to keep them placated lest the emperor have any reason to be concerned about his leadership and administrative skills. And here we see a problem that has been manifested in so much of our history: the unholy alliance of church and state and of the rich and powerful elites who seek to maintain and build their power at the expense of all others. This abuse of powers and exploitation of the weak has fueled generations of rebels and zealots in ancient history and in the present. It has fueled the anger and militancy of Marxists and other revolutionaries today—a blow torch of judgment and attempted radicalization that has often led to its own grotesque exploitation of the weak and powerless.

What makes the scene of the tomb poignant, powerful, and full of portent is how it played out, to the consternation and confusion of secular authorities and his own disciples. In that moment, the stone rolled away, and the guards—there at the command of the most powerful empire the world had yet known—were overwhelmed by the resurrection power of a Holy, active God. How symbolic and indicative that moment was for how God works—Christ did not come first and foremost to change the structures and institutions of humankind (much to the consternation of the people and even His disciples); He came to change the heart and to reconcile us back to God—to reacquaint us as sons and daughters to the One who made us and named us, who saw us before the dawn of time and is now calling us to Him (Ephesians 1:4-7). Christ ushered in a new work, a radical work because His love pursues us in our deepest heart of hearts. And in so doing, the human institutions, which have been so notoriously grinding along with continued exploitation, corruption, and abuse, are also caught off guard and upended, just as those guards were so caught off guard, confused, and overwhelmed when the stone rolled away on that epic and glorious morning so many years ago.

This book seeks to do justice to that powerful, resurrecting work of Christ. If it were solely a book on leadership, or the processes of government and society, it might busy itself, first and foremost, with the latest leadership theories, the history of political processes, the strategies of accomplished political leaders, and so forth. Certainly, we will focus on some of those things, but this book hopes to do more. For if Christ promised us an eternal well of water springing up into everlasting life (John 4:13-14), brought about by the infilling of the Holy Spirit and His transformative work in our hearts by the washing of the water by the Word (John 7:38, Ephesians 5:26-27), then we too should be captivated by that work, and seek to explain and understand how God, in His infinite wisdom, power, and love, seeks to gently transform us from the inside out, so that every area of human life, interaction, and society are also transformed, including those very oppressive structures that have often benefited by a corrupt alliance of Church and State.

We will see that this is a slow and deliberate process, often marred by human duplicity at worst, and frailty and foolishness at best, even among God's own children. But we will also see that despite all of that, God's work is faithful, and we should rejoice that in the end, He is not first and foremost concerned about transforming the structures, laws, and legal systems of society. He is first and foremost concerned about you and me. The tyranny of sin in the deepest, darkest, depths of our hearts is where the Lord starts. We are too precious and valuable to be seen as just a product of a systemic change or revolution. Thank God for that!

So, if the Lord works from the inside out—or more aptly stated, from the *eternal* (you and I, made in God's image) to the *temporal*—the foundations and structures of society, this book should do the same as it examines leadership and government strategies. We will certainly discuss major biblical themes such as covenant, inalienable rights, and the proper balance of Church and State in society, but we will first start with the implications of the Gospel for you and me as children of God, and then how we should relate to one another in the context of interpersonal relationships. From there, we will focus on how those very basic, and deeply intra- and interpersonal ideas manifest themselves in the broader context of society. To do that, we will review the history of how these ideas slowly reshaped and reformed society, not over years, but over centuries.

You see, Scripture reveals a God who is so patient in His work at more temporal, broader levels, not because He is apathetic, distant, or uncaring, but rather because He values so much our free-will and participation in His sovereign efforts. This statement is not an attempt to subject the reader to a debate about our free will versus God's sovereignty. But we should note that there is a high degree of mystery about how a sovereign God, outside of time and space, works with His temporal creation: in His providence, there is room for both His sovereign, initiating work, and our free will. As we will see, if we overlook that initiating work, we will fall prey to any number of idols of self-sufficiency and pride. So, God starts His work in our hearts, very patiently, and yes, very thoroughly. All manner of idols and bondages are exposed when we apply the Word of God to our brokenness. But the Gospel effects these changes in a loving, restorative way as we are introduced to the radical, alien holiness of God who also loves us tenderly and wholly.

On that point, this introduction opened with a mention of Pilate. Before he begrudgingly sent the guards to the tomb, before he caved into the Pharisees and to the people to beat and crucify Christ—before he did all of these things--he first put Christ on trial. He sought to examine His innocence: to determine if Christ truly was a radical zealot seeking to set up an earthly kingdom in rebellion to the Roman Empire. Christ said very little in that trial, but He did affirm that His was not a political kingdom (John 18:36) and that He came to testify to the truth (18:37).

It is at this point that we see the above-mentioned political power machine grind to a halt: "What is truth?" asks a cynical and frazzled Pilate (v. 38). Pilate was a man who lived and breathed the political intrigue and power plays that reside in any human empire, where words are mere fodder for the schemes of men to gain more power and where power—not ideals such as truth or justice—is the ultimate and perhaps only currency in the affairs of man. It is no wonder that he thought so little of the truth or at least was so perplexed by the question, confounded as he was by a difficult political situation in Jerusalem, perhaps exhausted by the constant passions of the people on matters small and great, trying to maintain his own sanity and authority while rivals doubtless worked against him. Who would ever know the truth in such a challenging situation, and even if the truth could be known, what would it matter when the machine—the system, the great empires of man—would roll over and grind anyone who stood in its way?

Pilate supposed that Christ was on trial—a politically engineered and capricious trial—but a trial nonetheless. And likewise, the Pharisees saw this trial as the outworking of their best political statecraft and God's approval. But in reality, Christ was not on trial; rather, we all were: scheming political and religious leaders, ignorant and easily impassioned people, braggadocios yet frail disciples, and an uncaring, oblivious world. We were all found guilty. In that moment, a perfectly righteous God could not bend any of His own righteous laws to save us; we had to be punished. But a perfectly loving God could not let us perish. It was His trial after all! His solution was to send His own son as fully God and fully man: a perfectly righteous substitute, not guilty of any sin who could stand in our place, so that we might be saved, and so that God's restorative work could continue in our very heart of hearts and work outward.

Hopefully this book will in some small way be a sacrament and testament to that eternal, holy, and loving work—the very gentle, intimate, and thorough work in our hearts and souls. This is the only way that true change and freedom occur, and the Lord is committed to it. Each chapter of this book, then, provides some guiding principles of how God approaches us and pursues relationship with us, and how that relational intimacy or lack thereof impacts our interactions with others in interpersonal relations, organizational behavior, and even matters of government and politics. It is vital that we start with the relational and heart level and work outward, or else even if we gain the whole world, we will have lost our souls. No political, social, or economic outcome is worth that. We are too valuable in the eyes of our loving Father. But if we let the Lord adopt us as His children, and surrender any claims of our own self-righteousness, power, and control, then not only can be we be radically freed and change at a heart level, but our relationships with others, our culture, our communities, and our society can be wonderfully transformed as well. This book will help you see that connection by first focusing on those divinely intimate principles that can free us from the slavery, rebellion, and orphanhood of sin and lead us into the loving arms of our heavenly Father. In Part I, we will see how this process profoundly alters and enlivens our relationships with others. Part II of the book then guides us in applying those same principles in the realm of professional behavior, organizational life, government, and politics and policy. Let's walk the path from the empty tomb to the freedom and truth that is waiting for every area of our lives.

PART I:
Intra- And Interpersonal Applications

CHAPTER 1
Heart of Hearts: The Realm of the Intrapersonal

Introduction

We have it all wrong; we think we must separate ourselves from the "outer world" of cares, concerns, and stresses to devote more time to our inner, spiritual lives, but that is not the reality. Rather, we start with a triune God who not only exists outside of time and space, but in fact, created time and space. This physical universe—despite its mind-boggling vastness and deep mysteries—is nothing more than a pocket of time and space in comparison to the eternal God. Therefore, this world is the inside, and our heart and souls, which were crafted in the image of God himself—are actually the "real" world—the external facet of our existence. Our hearts and minds stretch into eternity. But because we look at the world from the inside out—from the temporal first, usually at the expense of the eternal, we quickly default to self-sufficiency. Thus, we forget our need for God's grace.

This chapter focuses on some of those most dangerously simple truths about who we are in Christ in our very heart of hearts, and how embracing that Truth begins to reformat us from the eternal to the temporal. How we see God and His treatment of us determines how we see and treat ourselves, which in turn determines how we see and treat others. And here is the essential truth: *we were not made to earn God's favor; we were made to receive it, to live in it, and to share it with others*—all through the saving work of Christ. This is a simple, foundational truth, which takes a lifetime to understand and live out. But a lifetime of practice of this essential, Gospel truth is indeed a life lived well.

Who We Were: Rebels, Orphans, and Slaves

But the ability to live life well is hindered and obscured by our spiritual state of sin and death. Scripture indeed provides a comprehensively dismal picture of our spiritual state without Christ (Jeremiah 17:9, Mark 7:21-23). We were enemies of God (Romans 5:10), slaves to sin (John 8:34, Romans 7:14-24), and orphans without friend or family (Ephesians 2:3). Imagine all of that rolled into one—a sad picture of an angry, fearful, slave-orphan without recourse or hope, baring his teeth, snapping and growling at the One who might help. And not only that, but we were quick to hate on our fellow captives—to see that the chains of slavery chafed them too, and to rejoice when they fell under further punishment from the tyrant's whip.

This is not a pretty picture and seems especially harsh in light of the fact that people are made in God's image and therefore demonstrate morality and regard for others. It is made further difficult by the behavior of some of the most religious whose self-righteousness sets them apart as uniquely cruel, as Frederick Douglass regarded his most religious slavemasters.[1] But here again we must not look from the temporal to the eternal, but to the other way around—from the eternal to the temporal.

The God described by Scripture is not only eternal and timeless, but also Good. He is not just good, He *is* Goodness—love, justice, and beauty all wrapped up into a triune being whose perfect fellowship, joy, and truth are beyond comprehension (Psalm 31:19, 34:8, 84:11, 107:1, Jeremiah 29:11, John 3:16, Luke 18:19, James 1:17, I John 1:5, 4:8). It is this God who introduced himself to Moses as "I am that I am" (Exodus 3:14, John 8:48-59). He is the starting point for all truth and reality. If one deconstructs any sense of goodness, love, or justice, and peels back the layers of cultural assumptions, norms, and beliefs, if one traces the etymology of one word to another, back through history to the dawn of language, either everything unravels into nihilism, or you confront the One who always was, who always is, and who always will be, the One who by His very nature defines what is good. He is our reference point for all truth, meaning and goodness. It is no wonder that the guards quaked when Christ said, "I Am" (John 18:4-6).

So yes, in comparison to this "alien righteousness," our righteousness is indeed the equivalent of filthy rags (Isaiah 64:6). Anything less than perfectly good falls short, after all. The extent of this truth should keep any of us from being glib about it, whether in view of ourselves or others. And the problem is not even just that we commit sinful behaviors all of the time. The problem is that Scripture warns that sin itself is also a confounding, binding spiritual force which subverts our understanding of truth and goodness (John 8:34, Romans 7:17-28). This is why we are not only slaves to sin but also rebels at the same time, and why we are doomed apart from divine intervention. This is why Martin Luther, at first failing to understand the wonderful interrelation between faith and grace, and looking deeply and without hope at his own abiding sin, at first cursed God because he knew that he was doomed for this allegedly righteous and wrathful God.[2]

If there is no God, then all of our conversations about good and evil would be reduced to cultural and personal preferences, with, at best, an appeal that doing what is good for society is good for oneself. But if there is a God, specifically the God of the Bible who was not a product of the universe itself, but instead created the universe and all that is with it, our reference point for good and evil is wrested out of our hands and focused specifically on Him.

Fortunately, this God who could have been so far removed from us has made it plain what is good and evil, and how we can come to know it. He took on flesh as the divine *logos*,

---

[1] Lex Loizides, "Religious Legalism and Racism—Frederick Douglass," *Church History Review* (March 21, 2019), https://lexloiz.wordpress.com/2019/03/21/christian-legalism-and-racism-frederick-douglass/.

[2] Michael Waldstein, "The Spousal Logic of Justification: St. Thomas and Luther on Paul's Key Topic Statement Romans, 1:17," *Doctor communis* 1/2 (2009): 186.

the Living Word of God (John 1:1-5). That Christ was introduced to us by the Father in such a manner affirms three very important aspects of life and meaning:

1. He came as the Truth, which means He came to give us meaning. Do we not all struggle with trying to make sense of life? Why we are here, why things are so hard, and often, so bad, or when things are going well, why do we still feel empty? Christ came with answers to those questions.
2. He came as a human. Christ came as fully God (Luke 3:22, John 20:28, Titus 2:13) and fully man (Luke 2:7, Galatians 4:4, I John 4:2, 2 John 7), into this dreary and dusty world of minutia and hardship, where all of the small and insignificant people are often ground down by the systems of the rich and powerful. And moreover, He came as a carpenter, even though He was King. He came looking for all of the poor rebel, orphan-slaves which had been despised by society. He came for you and me, and that means that our lives have meaning and importance.
3. He fulfilled love and justice. What is a perfectly just, loving, and righteous God supposed to do with us—these frail rebel orphan-slaves? Imagine we are in a courtroom and He is judging each one of us, not just for our actions but our deepest and most hidden thoughts? Imagine being exposed thoroughly and fully—every thought and motive clearly and fully exposed for God's searing judgement. Can God overlook any of our sins? If He did He would be denying His own righteous laws and He would no longer be good. There is only one punishment for us—eternal banishment from all that is good (Ezekiel 18:20, Matthew 25:46, Romans 6:23, 2 Corinthians 5:10, James 1:15, 1 John 3:4) Because we are less than good—far less—how can we remain in the presence of Holy Righteousness (2 Thessalonians 1:9, Revelation 20:15)? But if He lets us die—if He lets us fall prey to that eternal banishment, how could His perfect love be said to be real and true? So, the only remedy is for God himself to step in: the Father sends the Son (John 3:16-18). As fully God, Christ lived a perfectly righteous life on earth (John 19:4, 2 Corinthians 5:21, 1 Peter 2:22, 1 John 3:5). Because of the incarnation, he was fully man, and therefore able to actually receive the punishment due all mankind (Revelation 20:11-15).

A brief aside here—this divine intervention is also a divine interruption. We were never looking for God; He came looking for us. Is that not the message of the prodigal son (Luke 15:11-32)? Both sons in fact were rebellious and conceited in their own ways, one in seeking a life of rabid self-pleasure and the other encasing himself in rigid and hard-hearted legalism. They both saw the Father as a means to an end. But still, their loving Father came looking for both. This does not overcome our free will and the need to choose; it just reminds us that we were never looking to choose Christ. He had to choose us first. We were still railing against him, on the slave trade block, while His blood paid our ransom (Ephesians 1:7, 1 Peter 1:18-19).

Given this state of affairs, it would be helpful to take a closer look at each of these descriptors. First, we are slaves. Sin entered the world through Adam and was passed to all of us (Romans 5:12-17, 1 Corinthians 15:21-22). The Bible describes us dead in sin—lost and hopeless (Titus 3:3-4). Living in a hurt and broken world has consequences—hurt people hurt people. Deep wounding leads to apathy, withdrawal, and addictive behaviors to cover up the pain and emptiness. We are controlled by the full spectrum of evil, addictive behaviors. For some, that is some sort of sexual or chemical addiction, but there are also a whole host of socially acceptable addictions. In fact, they can be a source of pride. Consider how the addiction of perfectionism has ensnared many with its lie that we can achieve some modicum of effectiveness and competence. We pursue this to the death of true intimacy with others, sometimes especially in Christian settings, where we will not live a truly confessional life with brothers and sisters in Christ for fear that we would be judged and despised. There is also the addiction of people-pleasing, where our efforts to care are wrapped up in a desperate need for acceptance and love.

Secondly, we are alone in this struggle—we are without intervention and aid from the One source who could intervene. We are without family, and we fight for any scraps we can on the crowded, chaotic streets of life. This insecurity leads to manipulative tendencies, fits of anger, prideful comparisons, and striving, always striving. The more we feel the need to prove ourselves, the less secure we are in God's love, and the more we need it.

Thirdly, we are rebels. We rebel by assuming our perceptions of reality, our feelings, our vanities, and our striving are all paramount. Even our self-doubt and loathing are themselves another type of addiction, because we are addicted to making pronouncements. We would rather serve as kings of despair than as servants and children of unmerited but unrequited love. Does all of this seem a bit melodramatic? Perhaps it is. Perhaps the normal routines of life do not really afford such dramatic confrontations with sin and warring in the spirits and souls of men. Or perhaps routines are just another addiction, another way to lure us to sleep with materialism, the cares of this world, and the small-mindedness of temporal concerns (Mark 4:18-19). Perhaps the well-worn paths of routine and leisure in our lives are themselves a slave's attempt to run away from the longings of his own heart—better to let the broken heart sleep than to be aware of its own complicity in its bondage.

How do we make sense of all of this? Consider that our hearts are shaped uniquely to hold God's love for us. It is the only thing that can fill that emptiness. Without God's love, one of two things can happen, as Stephen Mott argues.[3] The first is the idolatry of control—perhaps it is better said that we become addicted to control. An evidence of this addictive behavior and bondage is anger, and anger itself is connected to fear. Find a person who is easily angered about things, and you will find someone who is so desperate for control that they are easily undone when something is askew. In its extreme, this can lead this person to exploitation and manipulation of others. This is a product of feeling like an orphan, and not believing that God can be trusted. When one feels alone and abandoned, there can be a desperate need for control.

On the other extreme, orphanage syndrome can lead to a mindset where a person gives up any sense of self-government and abdicates. The end result is apathy and this too can be the beginning of dangerous addictive behaviors as a means of escaping the pain, all in an attempt to make up for the absence of God's love which belongs in the human heart. The

---

[3] Stephen Mott, *A Christian Perspective on Political Thought* (Oxford University Press, 1993), 31–33.

only recourse is surrender to Christ, not apathy, but the orphan has not yet learned to hear the Father's call. To some extent, we are all on this continuum between idolizing control or escapism, and it is probably reasonable to say that depending on the day and situation, we could be more of control addicts one moment and then succumb to escapism in the next.

In either case, we are insecure, because of the void in our hearts. Insofar as we feel alone, and must therefore do it all ourselves, we also become prideful and vainglorious. We prop ourselves up, which feeds our striving and impression management. Find a person who is boastful and prideful, and you will doubtless find a scared, insecure orphan child who has not yet learned the value of exchanging his rags and chains of self-sufficiency for the royal inheritance of God's love and grace. Pride and insecurity are two sides of the same coin.

If all of this is true, we might better understand why there is evil at all in the world. Why would a good and loving God even allow for such bondage and suffering? The answer is this: any parent knows the difference between a child who willingly runs into their arms versus one who only obeys out of compulsion, as the older son in the parable noted above did. God did not want robots—He wanted us to choose to love him and to enter into the joy and fellowship of the Holy Trinity. That was the only way. And now since Adam's fall, we live in a world of semi-darkness where our sin compounds upon itself from generation to generation—again because of the free will God has bestowed to us—and obscures our awareness of God's truth and light. But if our sin casts long shadows, it is ultimately because the crack of dawn awaits—the light that shines more and more unto the perfect day (Proverbs 4:18-19), the way of the righteous made possibly through Christ's finished work (Hebrews 10:19-21). Let us turn then to what He has done for us.

Who We Are: Vulnerability and Intimacy in Christ

To that end, let us look at five key Gospel doctrines: justification, redemption, reconciliation, adoption, and propitiation. These words are not the result of empty intellectualism; they are not the mere incantation uttered by old professors of theology in some medieval study. They are words that open up to us a deeper understanding of how much God loves us through His Son. Indeed, as an old pastor friend of mine said about them, they are all like windows looking into the same room. Each of these windows—justification, redemption, adoption, and propitiation—gives us a slightly different glimpse into the notion of the Gospel, but they are all related and useful in increasing our understanding. And indeed, it might be better said that they are not windows looking in, but rather looking out to freedom and joy that awaits us as we learn to leave our prison cell and walk into God's love. To examine this, it is helpful to start with a heavy task—understanding God's righteous and holy, and utterly consuming wrath.

Propitiation

The image of the angry god has been with us since humans first scraped together their human-made religions. We will contrast that image with the biblical image, but first, consider the counterfeit—angry, hungry gods whose desire for sacrifice and blood is never quite satisfied. And these gods are always so easily offended. We are left scrambling for ways to appease them and discern their will.

The angry god counterfeit has certainly infected Christianity too. Wherever there is an angry, self-righteous, legalistic Christian, there is someone who has not understood the biblical concept of propitiation. Because in Scripture, God's anger is perfectly just, clearly discernible, and fully and finally completed in the work of Christ. His anger toward sin is perfectly just because He is perfectly good; He is goodness itself (Proverbs 24:12, Matthew 25:46, Romans 2:5, 5:1). How dare we presume to do anything that would compromise or lessen perfect goodness! How dare we would presume to weigh our own hearts, to be our own judge, to question whether God truly has a complete grasp on notions of good and evil! And yet it is a socially and culturally accepted norm to "find our own truth."

Secondly, His righteous anger is clearly discernible. We have a written record of God's decrees from Old to New Testament (Jeremiah 30:23, Nahum 1:2, Romans 1:18, Revelation 19:15). The Bible itself is a collection of numerous separate books, written by numerous authors, over hundreds of years. The process by which the books of the Bible became established cannon is itself a testimony to how God works with human free will, despite all of its frailty, to achieve the ultimate truth of the Gospel. From God's covenant to Adam and Eve, to Noah, to Abraham, Isaac, and Jacob, then to Moses and David, we see a message that loving God and our neighbors with all of our hearts and souls is a goal that we can never attain in our own. The ceremonial and legal codes of Mosaic law were fulfilled by Christ on the cross (Hebrews 8:6-7, 9:25-26, 10:19-24), so that the moral components of the law—what it means to truly love God and love one's neighbor fully and completely can finally be written on our hearts (Jeremiah 31:33) and so that finally we can worship God and spirit and in truth (John 4:23-24). Our God does not seek sacrifices first and foremost—He does not demand abject and fearful worship, as if our frail worship could do anything to stroke His omniscient and almighty ego. Instead, He wants us to truly know him for all that He is—perfect love, justice and beauty, and in perfect fellowship with the members of the holy Trinity. When we know him for all that He is, the only response is loving worship.

And finally, we see that God's wrath was solely and completely fulfilled in Christ. Note that the Father was not on a tirade, such that the Son had to intervene and offer himself lest God send everyone to eternal damnation. Instead, what we see is the Father sending the Son on behalf of mankind. "For God so loved the world that he gave his only Son, that whoever believes in him should not perish but have eternal life" (John 3:16). So we see His anger was a perfect anger. It could have and should have been focused on us, but He showed mercy through His Son. But in Christ, what was once the blast of God's anger toward our sin has now become gentle breeze of God's grace, leading us to repentance (Isaiah 53:5-6, 10, Titus 3:5-6).

Justification

We start with the courtroom again—that solemn and fearful trial where by all rights we were doomed. Imagine that you are on trial and now every thought and motive of your heart has been exposed and discussed with painful specificity. Every action has been examined. You (and we) have fallen far short. Now, if you can take a moment to look up from your despair, take a glance at the heavenly Father—the righteous Judge. Mind you, Moses asked for this look and had to be hidden in the cleft of the rock as God passed by or else he would have been overwhelmed by God's full glory (Exodus 33:22), but we will allow for flexibility in our imagination here. If you could actually look upon the righteous Judge, you would not see anger, nor would you see the gavel banging the mantle to announce your doom. Instead, you would see this same righteous Judge calling forth His Son. Christ now offers himself as your sacrifice. The righteous Judge affirms the rightness and holiness of this act. It is perfect and complete—love and justice have been balanced in the cross—it is finished (Romans 3:21-26, 4:5-6, 1 Corinthians 1:30, 2 Corinthians 5:21, Galatians 2:16)!

This is why we do not look at our sin so much as we look at the finished work of Christ. Where legalism and works-based righteousness would seek to crush you into despair because you ever fall short, your legal advocate, the Holy Spirit (John 14:15-27, 16:5-11), would remind you instead that your debts have been paid, and not only for salvation, but for the rest of your life, as you learn to cling to Christ more and more. Did you think that the God who created time itself would only cover initial salvation? His work was complete and thorough and for all eternity and therefore for all of your life. That is why it is said that justification describes the work of Christ on the cross as the perfect legal remedy for our sin. The "accuser of the brethren" has nothing to say because this remedy is thorough, complete, and entirely in keeping with God's law (Revelations 12:10).

Redemption

The doctrine of redemption, meanwhile, is a natural extension of justification. Sin is slavery. Yes, it takes a great ransom to free us from slavery, but of course, it is an even heavier price to live a life of sin. So just as justification describes the cross as providing a legal remedy, redemption describes the cross as the means by which Christ paid our unpayable debt (Galatians 3:13, Ephesians 1:7, Hebrews 9:15, I Peter 1:18-19). Like the old song says,

I owed a debt I could not pay,
He paid a debt he did not owe.

This might not move the heart of a person who does not understand the depth of their own sin. On the other hand, there are many, like Luther, who are relieved beyond measure that the crippling debt which has hounded them for so long has finally been exorcised (Hebrews 2:14-15).

Reconciliation

In turn, where were once slaves, now we have become friends with God. To say that we are only friends with God through Christ is to say that before Christ, we were deep and abiding enemies of God (Romans 5:10, 2 Corinthians 5:18-21, Ephesians 2:14-16, Colossians 1:19-23). Even those of us who feel that we are pretty good on our own terms must admit that if God and God alone is perfectly good, then it is a foolhardy, pompous, and rebellious act indeed to pretend that we can determine and evaluate our own righteousness apart from God. But we certainly love to do so. And that perhaps explains why we are so keen to rebel.

Here is the rub: we are slaves to sin, so in some sense, our rebelliousness is truly a "false consciousness," to borrow a term from feminist critique. We think we are just fine on our own. It takes a divine intervention to realize the truth. So how does God reconcile the need to give us the space to be free–to choose, and at the same time to intervene so that we can actually be free to choose? This is an ancient question debated among theologians to this day, as well as college students stridently debating Arminianism versus Calvinism well past midnight.

But in the end, we cannot fully, truly fathom what a God who created time itself, acts freely to balance our need for divine intervention and free will. Scripture speaks to both—it speaks to us being dead in our sin and therefore being unable to choose. It speaks to the reality of first things and first orders—that repentance on our part does not come before regeneration and lead to it, but rather that regeneration—the act of coming alive with the new birth in Christ—leads to repentance (2 Corinthians 4:6, Ephesians 1:3-10).

But it also speaks of our relationship with God in covenantal terms, where we are offered a choice to compact with the God of creation and where we cannot be coerced. We will talk extensively of covenant further on in the book, but here it is introduced to show you that free will is very much a part of God's pursuit of us. He pursues us so gently—this divine intervention of His never comes with the slavemaster's rebuke or punishment. In Old Testament covenantal language, as God introduces covenantal terms to His people, we are told to hearken to Him—that is, to choose to listen. He will not even make us listen.

And yet, can we really listen if He has not opened up our ears to hear? There is no easy answer to this, but this: in the divine order in which we must rank God's sovereignty and our human free will, where both somehow mysteriously coexist, it makes much more sense to start with God's sovereignty and loving intervention. Somehow, there is still room for our free will. But what then of people who never follow Christ? It would be foolish indeed to say that God simply does not intervene in some people's lives, consigning them to death. We simply cannot say that, and it would be presumptuous to try to explain this. It is far better to be overcome with the mystery of how God, who loved the world so much that He sent His only Son, still saves us and yet gives us free will.

So here we are—complete and utter rebels, being chased by God. In discussing justification, you were offered the image of being a defendant on trial. Now consider yourself a rebel on the run, holing up in an old shack out in a rugged and harsh country. You are surrounded by God's holy deputies. They have you "dead to rights" as is said in old American Westerns. You cannot flee, and your old, dilapidated six shooter is out of ammunition—a fact of which your pursuers are well aware. And then comes Christ. He comes in love and peace. He shows you the holes in His hands, just as He did to Thomas (John 20:24-28). You realize He was not coming to take your life, but to give you life. He stands at the door and knocks (Revelation 3:20), and wonder of wonders, you finally let him in. It is over—you are no longer a desperate rebel, always on the run, always hunted. In fact, for the first time, you understand that you were only being chased by God so that you might be finally saved from the real predators of your heart—sin and all of its consequences. And yes, you might be a bit overcome, just like the prodigal son, that the prodigal Father came running for you. But you accept it; you allow him to take you in His arms. And this is where reconciliation so quickly leads to the doctrine of adoption.

Adoption

Here, you are no longer an enemy of God. You are no longer a slave to sin. Those previous dispositions had left you as a helpless, angry, fearful orphan. But no longer. Now, you are a beloved child of God (Romans 8:14-19, Galatians 3:26, 4:5-7, Ephesians 1:3-10, Hebrews 2:10-13). Finally. You are clothed in royal vestments, and given a royal inheritance, if only you will accept it through Christ—there is no other way (Matthew 11:27, John 14:6, Hebrews 2:14-15).

Illusions of Self-Sufficiency, Addictions, and Dehumanization

That is it: our cruel slavemaster would have had us continue life-long in our slavery, but the price was paid, and we are free. But do we really want to be free? Our rebel hearts might have other ideas, and even now, our old slavemaster peers at us from the shadows, scheming to bring us back in to the old ways. These were the ways He aspired to as well. To quote Milton's Lucifer: "Better to reign in hell then serve in heav'n." What a lie—the futility and depravity of sin leaves us nothing! We are in control of nothing, and we are dehumanized and objectified. But still our hearts are attracted to the shiny glint of a false promise—to have control, to have autonomy, to do things our own way, as our hearts see fit. This is the promise of our great and abiding Enemy. We all know the heart ache of continued striving, of running and running from the gentle urging of the Holy Spirit. Here is the freedom the Enemy promises us: the drug addict, in the streets, despised by family and friends, no longer able to function in society. Yes, he has his freedom—there are no more social restraints that might have kept him tied into loving obligation to others. He can pursue his addiction to the end.

Here is another picture of that freedom—the workaholic, legalist, perfectionist—always trying to earn it, always trying to be good at everything, always so easily undone by any hint of self-weakness. Working hours on end, because the work never ends, not having time for family, for little ones who might soften his heart, and he theirs, because there is always a bit more work to be done. Or we can look at the worrier—the one who will not bow the knee to trusting God with every detail, and therefore tries to manage every detail on her own. Is any of this real freedom? Yes, it is a freedom of sorts—freedom from Christ's loving intervention. But there the freedom ends, and all we are left with is the tyranny that first shackled the hearts and minds of Adam and Eve. And eventually, if we continue in this so-called freedom, we only have depravity and futility to show for it. Eventually, as Romans 1:24-32 promises us, God will give us up to depraved minds if we persist in our rebellion. Sin, then, is its own punishment. The things we so long for, we often get, but never in the ways about which we had fantasized. The question is whether we will stay in that freedom or revert back to the illusion of autonomy and control. It is the abiding temptation, and the moment we succumb to it, is the moment we fall into the old ways—striving, competing, worrying, and self-absorption.

Healthy Vulnerability

What a contrast—the harshness of soul-crushing sin with all of its slavery contrasted with the Father's gentle pursuit of us through Christ! The Gospel impacts who we are as seen above, and also how we interact with others. Since "the One who knows us the most loves us the most," we can be real about our struggles and imperfections—we do not have to adopt a fake persona for fear of being discovered—of being truly known, and therefore being rejected. We can own our shortcomings, seek forgiveness when needed, and forgive others. We can divest ourselves of the burden of impression management and instead love people without condition.

It is an amazing thing to realize that since we could not earn God's favor anyway, and since He loves us unconditionally, that we are free to love others and engage with them without any strings attached. This is easier said than done, because there is the very real struggle of being rejected by loved ones—parents, siblings, spouses, and friends. Hurt people hurt people, after all. But the Gospel reminds us that we can love others unconditionally only by remembering that we are loved unconditionally in Christ. It takes faith to remember this, grace to meditate on it and abide it.

If this describes you, it is hoped that the content does not come off as smarmy or manipulative, truly. That is one of the challenges of trying to write through this content. There is perhaps nothing more damaging to great truths than to convey them poorly, or glibly. I would just ask that if this indeed part of your story—whether it be parents, or siblings or whomever, that you could look at those hurtful people as those who once were hurt too. They were or perhaps, sadly, still are rebel orphan-slaves. They need to hear the call of their Savior, they need His hands to gently lead them off the slave auction's block and into the royal palace where they will always be loved. But while you should never pretend it did not hurt, and while you should never ignore actions which were criminal, I hope you hear Christ call you gently and remind you that you are His. He died for you, and that past hurt does not need to own you anymore. You are no longer a slave.

Listen to me. . . I'm a father, and at the time of this writing, I have seven beautiful children who are still young enough to call me daddy, and who enjoy punches and tickles, hug piles and wrestling, and, perhaps most importantly to me, cuddling. Maybe you did not have a father who loved to hold you tight and kiss your cheeks, but I promise you as a father, that if my love for my children is any indication—and it is—then you can rest assured that your heavenly Father wants to hold you tight and to heal you. He loves you so fiercely and tenderly, if He was willing to send His Son for you, will you not let that be enough for you, to sustain you, to fill your broken heart up, to remove your fear and anger, and to break off the bonds of slavery inflicted by other wounded slaves?

Therefore, consider two summative truths: first, healthy vulnerability is based on God's unconditional love. This gives us strength and freedom to love others unconditionally. This includes the confession of sin and learning to cling to Christ together. It also includes emotional self-awareness and being mindful and caring of others' emotional states as well. But secondly, healthy vulnerability does not idolize emotional connectedness to others. It is one thing to care for others and to allow them to care for you; it is another thing all together to be so desperate for that emotional connection that we force intimacy on others where it does not exist or when we allow our own emotions to be manipulated by others. We can avoid these pitfalls if we let God's love fill our empty hearts. We can be strong and love unconditionally, and though it may hurt when people do not love us back, we learn to give that hurt to the Lord. This is different from trying to shut off our emotions all together to try to hide the pain. This is not strength; it is rather the slow dying of our hearts. God is our source, not the fickle affection of others.

Then what is true strength? It can be a physical concept, but it certainly does not start there, nor should it end there. It is not a gender specific attribute—men and women alike can possess this attribute. Therefore, it is not about hyper masculinity or any other such silliness (but if you want to pump some iron, run some marathons, or unleash the hook shot against your opponents on the basketball court, etc., etc., by all means do so, but as an act of worship and joy in the Lord, and not for self-glorification).

Strength is the ability to both be emotionally vulnerable and intimate with others while also not being controlled by one's emotions or desperately needing the approval of others. It is knowing that God's love and approval through Christ are enough so that we in turn can love others unconditionally, knowing that people will never love us back perfectly, just as we cannot love others perfectly. It is knowing that unconditional love does not involve enabling the destructive, manipulative abusive behavior of others but rather confronting it (and in the worst-case scenarios, involving law enforcement). It is doing one's duty regardless of the cost, knowing that the love and joy of the Lord are our strength, not circumstances, not the approval of others, not even our own emotional disposition. Doing one's duty does not require us to "toughen up," to "grin and bear it," but it does require self-government and an understanding that while we are wonderful emotional beings, *we are not to be controlled by our emotions*; rather, the objective truth of God's Word always mediates and drives our subjective feelings.

Further, strength is gentleness—the use of restraint in contrast to uncontrolled force. We are not strong if we cannot control ourselves and our emotions. We are not strong if we are overcome by our own anger. It does not involve hardening your heart so that you do not feel pain anymore. It does not involve divesting from personal relationships with others due to hurt and disappointment (that will always happen, just as we will always hurt and disappoint others, even on our best days). Rather, it derives from a focus on quiet contentment and surrender in the Lord so that you do not miss out on His approval, joy, and love. This true, abiding strength. God's unconditional love is indeed enough . . . if we let it be enough.

Christian Perfectionism/Legalism: A Question of Who Gets the Glory

But will we let it be enough? It takes complete and total surrender to Christ. And as noted above, our former slavemaster is always looking for ways to ensnare us again, to keep the chains on. As we learn to recognize how we are participating with him to keep those chains on, we can grow and, yes, evolve into what Christ has for us. However, recognizing those chains is quite the task as our Enemy is always so subtle. In fact, here is one of the most duplicitous chains of bondage: *Christian perfectionism and legalism*. These are chains that we often gladly wear, as if they were jewelry worn to our finest engagements with others (especially church) when in reality they are cruel and debased entrapments. In short, Christian perfectionism/legalism is the falsehood that *we must earn our own sanctification and spiritual growth through our own human effort, and thus we have the right to be proud of our accomplishments rather than giving the glory to God.*

It is our own infatuation with pride and control, as if we were still orphans that makes this particular ensnarement so powerful. We want the credit and the glory. The fact that we are supposedly being a good Christian as we engage in this legalism makes the bondage even more enchanting, because we can enshroud our striving and our pride in Christian imagery and receive accolades from other Christians because we are seen as so virtuous. But what a trap this is because we do not actually engage in true growth—performance may be a fruit of the Spirit, but often it is a fruit of pride and self-sufficiency. Remember the comments above about what it means to be healed from past emotional hurts, especially those earned while growing from childhood to adulthood. Peter Scazzero argues that dealing with these past hurts and pains in a Christ-centered, healing way is the only way to grow spiritually—spiritual and emotional health are intertwined.[4]

Sadly, Christian perfectionism denies this growth and self-awareness because it only emphasizes actions, specifically those that can be seen by others. Any attempts to truly open up about past or present hurts and sins is seen as a weakness. In contrast, we know that healthy vulnerability is actually a strength and that staying closed off is sign of weakness and pain. Further, Christian perfectionism reduces sanctification to a checklist of sins that allegedly can be easily addressed with enough human will power and effort. But again, this is pride, and fighting any sin in this manner is akin to fighting fire with gasoline.

The offshoot is that in turn, when we do stumble yet again, Christian perfectionism then leads to self-condemnation. Tragically and ironically, self-condemnation is just hidden pride, because we are so self-absorbed that we focus only on our sin. God's grace and inherent standard of righteousness is, apparently, not sufficient, not fine-tuned enough. No, the work of Christ on the cross was not sufficient, we apparently must punish ourselves a bit. This is the trap of self-sufficiency and Christian perfectionism. The tragedy of this continues because of the fallacy behind our self-condemnation. The presence of just one sin belies the fact that the problem is much greater than just that one struggle.

Christian legalism and perfectionism mandate a solution to the problem of sin by focusing on our actions, such as the Bible more, praying more, and above all "trying harder." But we have to see that this is another trap, where we subvert God's initiating and sustaining grace in the name of earning God's favor through our own efforts. Many Christians have been slayed by this falsehood and in turn have been complicit in ensnaring others. The only remedy is to recognize that God always initiates change in us. Are you praying more and reading the Bible more? Good! That was the work of the Holy Spirit. Are you more aware of sin and bondage in your life? Excellent! Do not let the old striving, pride and

---

[4] Peter Scazzero, *Emotionally Healthy Spirituality* (Grand Rapids, MI: Zondervan, 2017), 20–21.

condemnation—all symptoms of Christian legalism/perfectionism—lead you to be afraid, ashamed, or crushed by that awareness. Instead, remind yourself that you are only aware of that sin because the Holy Spirit is working in your heart and it is time for more change.

What Are We Saying Yes To?

To that end, the Master Physician, Jesus Christ sent the Holy Spirit to aid us in our walk and fight against sin. The Spirit in turn draws us to meditate in the Word of God. We learn to rest in God's unconditional love. We learn that we are not just saying no to a particular sin; rather, we are also saying yes to God's love and intimacy. Christian perfectionism and legalism knows nothing of this sweet intimacy and vulnerability in Christ. It only knows that we should avoid sin. It can only say no, and thus it fails. The pride of accomplishment, the accolades of others is rarely enough to overcome sin, particularly addictive behaviors, and even if it were enough, it itself is its own addictive, sinful behavior. But true Christianity learns to say yes to intimacy—that is the only antidote to the intensity of addictive behaviors. Be loved by God, rest in Him, abide in Him (John 15:1-17).

This is the only way to find joy and to realize that we say no to sin not to avoid self-condemnation, the reproach of others, or even the consequences of sin; no, the main reason we lean to say no to sin is so that we can say yes to the joy of abiding in Christ. Again, God's unconditional love is indeed enough . . . but only if we let it be enough. Say yes to God's unconditional love. The next chapter builds upon these truths as we further examine the biblical idea of covenant and its impact in history and interpersonal relationships. Healthy interpersonal relationships are predicated on a healthy relationship with the God.

CHAPTER 2
Covenant and Interpersonal Relationships

Introduction

Imagine for a moment, a nearly impossible thing—the Trinity. God the Father, God the Son, and God the Holy Spirit, in perfect fellowship before time even existed. A state of mutual celebration, mutual submission, and perfect joy. A love so pure, so holy, so perfect that it desired to share itself with us, God's most cherished creation, not out of loneliness, for in the Trinity there was already prefect fellowship. Not out of a selfish desire to be worshiped, for again, in the Trinity, perfect, mutual celebration already existed, and after all, we were given free will so that worship could not be coerced, in any case. Only out of a true, selfless love—a love that understood before creation itself that a selfless sacrifice would be needed to truly reconcile man and God. From this near fantastic image, we see hints of what human fellowship could be, and should be.

Could be and should be, but often not is. The world is both desperate for true intimacy and quick to either idolize it or despise it when it happens. We spent the first chapter examining the boundaries of who we were made to be and how our individual heart and souls were made to be in perfect fellowship with this wonderful God, but only through Christ and the saving grace of God. We now will try to extrapolate those ideas into what human relationships can be if they are patterned after the love and glory emulated by the Holy Trinity. This would be a ridiculous task to conceptualize, much less walk out, except that Christ has already walked out of an empty tomb to give us hope.

The biblical idea of covenant provides a powerful unifying theme for understanding what healthy relationships should look like both interpersonally and in organizational and political settings and moreover, for understanding what it means to live in fellowship with others, as modeled by the Trinity. A covenant is a mutually affirming, long-term relationship based on mutual care and accountability and a pledge to love one another. In Scripture, God is seen as either the one introducing and initiating the covenant, or the one who affirms each covenant member's roles and duties when entering a covenant. The idea of covenant is indeed one of the major themes of Scripture; in fact, a better translation for Old and New Testaments is Old and New Covenants, as will be seen below.

The Theology of Covenant

To say that covenant is an abiding theme in Scripture is to emphasize that God does not coerce people into a relationship with Him. He urges them to "hearken"; that is, to choose to listen to His proposal.[1] He promises them covenant love (*hesed*), which effectively means to go beyond the letter of the law in fulfilling God's promises to us.[2] And of course, it also implies that when we fail our end of the covenant, that God directs the punishment we deserve onto Himself, through Christ.

Also, the covenantal nature of Scripture is seen in how one covenant affirms and supersedes previous covenants. This reveals two themes about God's character. First, it affirms that God's character is indeed the same today, yesterday, and forever (Hebrews 13:8). He is not a fickle, capricious, angry God. He does not go back on His word and He does not forget his promises (Numbers 23:19, Matthew 24:35). Secondly, the covenantal nature of Scripture reveals that God himself has always been working throughout human history to bring forth this covenantal relationship, which, in our own strength and goodness, we would never attain. This was why the serpent's head was crushed by the Messiah (Genesis 3:15), why Noah was promised that mankind would have mercy and not punishment (Genesis 9:8-17), why Abraham saw the flaming pot walk between the slain animals (Genesis 15:17), why Moses was taught all of the sacrificial, moral, and ceremonial laws, why David was promised a divine posterity (2 Samuel 7:4-17), and why all who put their hope in Christ's salvific work were grafted into the tree of Abraham (Romans 11:11-31). We see in Scripture a covenant-keeping God intervene on behalf of covenant-breaking mankind. We see the Good Shepherd become the sacrificial lamb (Isaiah 53:7, John 1:29, 36, 1 Peter 1:19), and then become our great High Priest (Hebrews 7:24-25). It is finished; the covenant promises have been fulfilled! And the punishment we should have earned for breaking the covenant, akin to being cut in two like the Abraham's severed animals, was instead directed at Christ; only God walked among those severed animals while Abraham observed.

Hesed: In Spirit and in Truth

The key operative mechanism of a covenantal relationship is *hesed*, which means "loving fulfillment of covenant obligation." It is the concept of hesed that most meaningfully distinguishes a covenant from a contract. A contract is clearly and only a *quid pro quo* relationship; exchanges are made on a limited basis. A covenant, meanwhile, is a long-term relationship promising mutual love and accountability. In a contract, legalists and fellows of ill repute look for grey areas in the contractual language, which is why most formal agreements in society are overcome and overburdened by legalese and fine print in an attempt to prevent such chicanery. In fact, find a society who has forgotten the Golden Commandment to love one's neighbor as oneself, and you will find a society that is obsessed with the fine print. In contrast, *hesed* is

---

[1] Daniel Elazar, *Covenant & Polity in Biblical Israel* (New Brunswick, NJ: Transaction Publishers, 1995), 70–71.

[2] Elazar, *Covenant & Polity*, 71.

all about going the extra mile to care for the other members of the covenant (Mathew 5:41). In short, *hesed* assures that love and duty are intertwined as the foundation for the relationship.

On that note, we seem to have a problem with such a fusion. We often fall prey to the fallacy that if we truly love and care for someone, duty will never exist. If we feel, on the other hand, that it is our duty, then the relationship must be bereft of love, because after all, duty is dry, loveless, and consumed by rote drudgery. We are so afraid of "going through the motions" in relationships such that we are never content and are apt to look longingly into hypothetical relationships with others—other spouses, other churches, other friends, etc. To the extent that this is a problem for us, it is because we are always looking for fulfillment in human institutions and relationships when in fact only the love of God through Christ can fill that God-shaped hole in our hearts. Until we learn this, we will be prone to chase our tails; we will ever chase the intensity of the new experience—the new relationship—the next infatuation, and thus we will never be at rest. And in doing all of this, we find that we exploit others, because we so desperately need them to be what they can never be; they can never be God Himself. Or we will allow ourselves to be exploited by those people because we have put them on a pedestal and we are unable to stand on our own two feet and walk away from harmful relationships.

Happily, the biblical idea of covenant frees us from this endless pursuit of meaning. We are reminded that the first and final relationship is with God through Christ. Christ fulfilled *hesed* for us on the cross, so that we can indeed worship God in spirit and in truth, as Jesus promised in John 4:23-27. In Christ, we discover that we were meant to experience intimacy and vulnerability, since we see that "the One who knows us the most loves us the most." Whereas in our own strength, we engage in constant impression management or unhealthy vulnerability with others, in Christ we discover that there is no more hiding, and that we must learn to accept unconditional love. This in turn allows us to unconditionally love others, and to no longer idolize the inconsistent and unreliable approval of others. To the extent that we idolize this approval, we undermine and devalue the love and affection of the most beautiful and wonderful entity within and beyond the universe. It is sad that we do this so quickly and easily.

Meanwhile, speaking of love and duty, we are reminded that part of loving someone is fulfilling one's duty to them. Yes, it is duty and it is also routine, but it is also a joy to fulfill it. And if something is important, do we not make it a routine? Some people run from routines because they know, intuitively, that life is not enough (and it is not). Finding the contentment that only comes from the Lord ensures that in fact we can find contentment and joy in the routines and duties of life as well.

Mutual Empowerment, Appreciation, and Accountability

With a *hesed* comes a sense of mutual empowerment and mutual appreciation. A covenant requires empowerment and freedom—no one can be forced into a covenantal relationship, either with God or with other humans. A covenant requires that each member of the relationship respect other and be respected by others. In this way, a covenant protects our rights even as we seek to protect the rights of others. Of course, this is only possible because of the spirit and impetus behind covenant—*hesed*: loving fulfillment of covenant obligation. So, in a covenant we empower one another, in part because we recognize that everyone else in the covenant has their own gifts and strengths to offer. For instance, in a marriage, the husband and wife recognize that love and respect go hand in hand, just like love and duty. This would be true of all manner of covenantal relationships, even though a marriage covenant is the deepest and most intimate of all human covenantal relationships.

Of course, every strength is also a weakness. Part of being in a healthy covenantal relationship is having the humility to recognize this pairing of personal strengths and weaknesses, and the grace to see that the weaknesses of others in the relationship usually are hiding a strength that is needed for healthy and successful interactions. Our ability to be gracious with one another is highly dependent upon our recognition that we have received abundant, overwhelming grace from the One who knows us well enough to convict us thoroughly of sin, pride, and hubris, but instead loves us unconditionally and tenderly through Christ. The rebel orphan-slaves have been forgiven much and have been extended covenant grace. So, we extend grace and empowerment to others.

And in so doing, we are accountable to others in the covenant relationship. This is healthy vulnerability—we are not desperate for the approval of others, nor are we callous to their needs, having put of a wall of defense. This defensive posture is indicative not of strength, but of a wounded heart that has decided that the best option is to prevent emotional vulnerability rather than risk, hurt, and pain. But a heart healed by God's grace is ready for healthy vulnerability and the mutual accountability that comes with it. And when this happens, the covenantal relationship—be it a marriage, a ministry team, a business, or even some facet of society—thrives and grows.

Empowerment and Collaboration

This growth comes because the members of the covenant develop a mutually respectful and affirming relationship with one another. And yes, they love one another. This may sound too idealistic and smarmy for something like a business team, but it is all covered by Christ's commandment to love one's neighbor as oneself. So covenantal love can and should cover every human relationship. A healthy covenantal relationship involves what can often feel like grueling conflict resolution. Most of humans either shy away from conflict or embrace with the relish of a barbarian horde sweeping down upon a defenseless village. There often is no in-between, but often one extreme response facilitates the other.

For example: instead of dealing head-on with misunderstandings and complaints, people gossip about others. Anyone who hears one side of the story is of course sympathetic to their friend's interpretation of events. They express sympathy and shock that the other person would act in such a way. When we play this role of the sympathetic (but often naïve) friend, we only exacerbate the anger and often uncharitable misinterpretations that fueled the anger. The anger in turn leads to an outburst and any number of related peace-breaking conflicts. As the gossip spreads, some people withdraw from the relationship. Others accuse and malign. People on all sides of the conflict become offended, and words increase in harshness and stringency. Anger begets anger, gossip begets gossip, and the Father of Lies, the great accuser of the brethren, laughs all along the way.

But covenant-keeping requires a different approach. It requires the humility to avoid "weaponizing" one's perceptions—that is, assuming that one's perceptions and interpretations of people's actions and intentions are correct—and giving them space to hear the other side of the story. What a problem this is—this weaponizing of perceptions! We think we have the right of it, and thus we share our perceptions of the situation with sympathetic friends and innocent bystanders alike with the full confidence of an innocent victim or righteous prophet. We of course forget that the prophets were speaking via a divine connection with God Himself, rather than the relying on their own perceptions. We forget to check our own biases and self-righteousness. It requires further humility to not take offense, but instead to listen first, speak second. It takes humility to quell rather than stoke fire of anger and fear that comes with conflict and communication breakdown and is carried forth in the flames of gossip and slander. But that is what is required with covenant keeping. It also requires covenant love—*hesed*—to see that what often appears to be divergent opinions and what appear to be competing principles must often be balanced rather than chosen one or the other. We often find ourselves on one side or the other, and sometimes the sides are clearly black and white, but often the sides are defined as good and important and "also good and important." A covenantal approach helps us work together, ensure accountability to one another and care for one another, so that we can balance these sides and moderate them when one perspective or the other is over-emphasized at the expense of the other "good and important" perspective.

Wonderful, Beautiful Boundaries

In the end, this is what covenant does for us—it provides boundaries that we would not normally want. We think we want absolute freedom, only to realize that this freedom leads to addiction, dehumanization, impression management, perfectionism, isolation, and death. We think we want complete intimacy with others only to realize that we have put others on a pedestal—a place of worship reserved only for God. The gospel of Jesus Christ offers us a covenantal understanding of relationships, where we learn that God uses human relationships to encourage us to follow Christ, to say no to sin, and to let the Holy Spirit moderate and grow the unique gifts that God has given us (Hebrews 3:12-14). In turn, the Holy Spirit also refines and unifies whatever part of the body of Christ we are in, as he draws us close to the Lord and to one another (John 14:26, 15:26, Romans 8:26, 15:13, Ephesians 5:26-27).

Being in covenant with others requires faithfulness, patience, love, and an eternal view. There is a price to pay for having meaningful, covenantal relationships with others. It does limit our options and our freedoms. It does require that we go through the process of thoughtful self-examination with those who love us enough to graciously point out possible weaknesses. But the rewards can lead to personal growth, meaningful, Christ-centered relationships, and impacts that stretch into eternity. We see then that while these covenantal ties and boundaries may limit us, they only do so in the sense that they limit us from our worst tendencies. We see then that they focus us and direct us to who were meant to be in Christ.

They are part of our eternal inheritance as sons and daughters of God. Only rebel orphan slaves are bereft of these.

The ties that bind,
Are the ties that strain,
Are the ties that sing life's sweet refrain.

Eternal principles, eternal impacts; all of these derive from the covenantal ties that bind us but also guide us and focus us. It will be argued throughout the rest of this book that these same covenantal principles are quite relevant and important for all facets of life, including government, politics, and society. But first, in the next chapter, we will examine covenantal principles in the realm of church life and conflict resolution.

God's Family, Your Family

In God's pursuit of us through Christ's work, we encounter a gentle but thorough and persistent effort on the part of the Holy Spirit to expose sin and bring life to every facet of our heart and soul. Often, as Hebrews 12:11 promises, this work can be uncomfortable and even painful. But it is always restorative and meant for our good, if only we are willing to persist and hold fast to God's promises that discipline occurs because He loves us (Hebrews 12:5-6) and that this work of discipline will yield good fruit in our lives. There is no condemnation in the work of Christ in our hearts (Romans 8:1-2). In fact, God's loving pursuit of us is a stark and abounding rebuke to the legalistic, judgmental ways we lay on one another, is it not? If true, there are some hypotheticals worthy of pondering.

Beautiful Imaginations

Imagine Christ-centered friendships where we pursue one another, as the Word commands us (Hebrews 3:12-14) and help each other overcome sin. Imagine your friends pursuing you in this gentle manner because they love you, not because they are angry with you. Imagine that instead of hurling accusations against you, which is an old habit learned from the Accuser of the Brethren, that instead they ask questions about observations of your behavior—they are too aware of their own sin to make judgments of your motives, but instead provide feedback for you that might help you better understand your own actions and yes, even your own motives. Imagine knowing that God loves you so much that you are not afraid to peel back the layers of self-justification and rationalization that so often keeps us from even being aware of sinful motives, and in turn, imagine being surrounded by like-minded brothers and sisters in Christ who are aware of their own self-deception and prideful tendencies. Imagine that these dear friends of yours are just as eager to receive loving exhortation from you as they are to give it, that all of this exhortation and observation-sharing is done out of love, for love does pursue, whereas selfishness tends to withdraw from the realm of conflict and deep, heart-level engagement. Imagine then that even conflicts and misunderstandings—the common currencies of living life together—are seen as an opportunity to cling to Christ together, to confess sin to one another, and to fight sin together.

The obvious overuse of the verb *imagine* here occurs because for too many of us, these types of friendships, at this depth of love and intimacy, does not occur. It cannot occur in a culture and atmosphere of Christian legalism and perfectionism, both of which are eagerly nourished by our own grand illusions of self-sufficiency. But I have most certainly seen it occur in an environment where God's sovereign grace is exposed faithfully from the pulpit. I have experienced it, and it is the greatest gift I have ever known as a Christian outside of the Gospel itself and my marriage. When the overwhelming love of God as He pursues us is communicated among believers, from the pulpit to the pews and then into the many informal interactions believers should be having with one another, you will find a lot of talk about sin, because there is even more talk about a sovereign, righteous, and loving God—the latter requires the former. But it occurs in the context of much joy about what Jesus Christ has done for us on the cross.

In turn, you will begin to understand that the confession of sin is a moment of great joy, because understanding our sin requires the work of the Holy Spirit to convict us. We do not discover our sin through our own volition, so conviction (a far differing process than condemnation) means that the Lord is at work, freeing us from the slavery of sin! Is that not a different look and feel from what we typically think of in other legalistic contexts, where discussions of personal shortcoming is often encased in judgment, self-condemnation, and discouragement? I have had the privilege of walking through this process of grace and growth with other brothers and sisters who have rejoiced with me as I have grown in Christ and who have been my long-suffering friends on the long journey of sanctification. They have seen the best of me because they have glimpsed God's love and faithfulness, and I have seen the best of them—not a finished work, but an ongoing work by a faithful Father who loves his children. Conversations and interactions with these friends have led to a rich a meaningful church life—true church and not some rigid idea of a church institution or building—where conversations were not shallow but quickly moved into deeper topics about the Lord's work in our lives through circumstances, hardships, and struggles. And meanwhile, despite all of this talk about sin and pride, I never experienced a more encouraging group of believers who were quick to point out God's work in my life, and the use of the gifts God had given me. You see, when a body of believers embraces the truth that we really are children of God, and we really can walk away from the ways of the rebel orphan slave, truly wonderful friendships of great depth can abound. We are not competing for encouragement or recognition, because we have learned that are all in need of grace but also are all fearfully and wonderfully made.

You may not believe this, but I can only say that I have experienced it—glimmers of joy and glimpses of eternity—worships services in Church full of passionate joy about the work of Christ, tears shed over the truth of Christ pursuing us, and the healing work that comes as the Holy Spirit refines us—this is all meant to be a communal and covenantal experience, and abiding one. This is the true Church, and the gates of Hell will not prevail against it. It does not happen often in this weary life, but when it does, it is a truly sacred and wonderful thing. It should happen more often, and would if we would remember our adoption in Christ.

As for those friends of mine, in times past and present, who have persisted in walking this path of covenant and grace with me, I offer you my thanks and love. Thank you for being a picture of the Father's love to me. You are worthy of what the Psalmist said in Psalm 16:3:

As for the saints in the land, they are the excellent ones, in whom is all my delight.

Husbands and Wives, Parents and Children

These same ideas should certainly be manifest in biological family life as well. Sadly, perfectionism and legalism, slavery and rebellion, all first bloom in the soil of how spouses fail to love one another, and how parents fail to love children. The relationship between a husband and wife is supposed to be one of the safest and deepest relationships we have, for our spouses truly see both the worst and best of us along with all of our unique eccentricities. And of course, it is often for those very reasons that our spouses are the ones who become our most effective enemies and a portal to the accusations and condemnations of our Enemy.

But again, imagine the fellowship described above occurring between a husband and wife, where despite being intimately aware of the unique and persistent brokenness we each possess, instead of judging and hating one another, we instead say, "This is not the truest part of you anymore—you are a new creation in Christ." Imagine that bringing conflict and concerns to one's spouse includes personal confession of sin for any unfair judgments and interpretations one spouse may have made of the other. My wife and I have learned that being offended may be the result of, first and foremost, being judgmental and unkind in assumptions that we make about one another. On the other hand, even if one spouse struggles with being judgmental, that does not free the other spouse from considering that their actions might also be unkind and unhelpful, and that motivations for behavior might also be selfish and indicative of bondage and sin.

Husbands and wives are supposed to help one another, to love one another, and to keep one another safe from the ravages of sin and temptation. Confession of our deepest struggles and motivations should be common, even, I think, struggles against sexual impurity and fantasies (both genders struggle with this, but often in different ways). Confessions keep the heart soft, and confessing sins to a spouse can provide us a much deeper awareness of our own sinful tendencies. In turn, confessions give our spouses the opportunity to point us back to Christ and his faithful and patient work in our lives. With these truths in mind, it is easy to see how conflicts themselves are a means of grace and a gift from a sovereign God who wants to deepen the relationships of husbands and wives with one another and with their loving Father. Further, husbands and wives are uniquely equipped to see how personal weaknesses are also strengths on the other side of the coin. We should be celebrating our spouses' strengths and having compassion on them as they struggle with their weaknesses. It seems too that these personal, besetting sins often manifest by gender and thus can lead to greater misunderstanding, conflict, and hurt because we do not always fully understand the struggles and affinities of the opposite gender. But bridging that gender gap can also be an opportunity for deeper growth and understanding.

Meanwhile, our greatest personal addictions—those enemies that seek to dehumanize us, steal our souls, and to lead us back to the slave auction's block—are also often manifest in marriage, often tragically so. For instance, a man who struggles with workaholism or sexual addiction will uniquely hurt his wife and by extension his children. Both are the fruits of the same diseased tree. It takes courage and faith in God for a man to learn to confess his sins in this area to his wife, just as it takes courage and faith on the part of the wife to hear those confessions, and to join in battle with their husband to fight those sins, and to realize that struggles in these areas are not a reflection on them, for no woman could ever fully satisfy a man, unless he is first satisfied in God's love, just as no man could every fully meet the romantic expectations of any woman, unless that woman is first content in her heavenly Father's love. And it takes wisdom for both the husband and wife to realize that the real struggle against those addictive behaviors is not about some nebulous sexual satisfaction or career fulfillment, but rather recognizing that in our heart of hearts, we do not believe that intimacy with Christ is enough—that we are not enough as fully developed humans made in God's image.

Here too we could discuss how women, as professionals, homemakers, and mothers, can become addicted to the perception others have of them in those roles—the "hostess with the mostest" is probably a phrase first chiseled out in Hell. In the case of either gender, there is an abiding and damning commonality: we run from vulnerability and intimacy and flee to addictive behaviors, all of which dehumanize us and measure us solely by what stimuli we are able to experience or how we are able to perform. These are complicated issues, my friends, and we must tread carefully. Confessions to our spouse keep the heart soft, but only if we receive and engage in those confessions as children of our loving Father. If in particular, my above discussions of gender do not resonate with you, please forgive me—I am not trying to put anyone in a stereotypical box; I am musing based on my own life experience. Do not mind me.

As for those of us who are parents, we know too well the dangers of perfectionism and legalism with our children, who by virtue of being our children, are unfairly pulled into our self-perceptions and expectations. It can be easy to want our children to act and behave a certain way—especially in public—to fulfill our own unrealistic expectations of control and perfection. And when they do not meet these unrealistic expectations, it can in turn be easy to hurl down condemnations from our Christian legalistic perch. Discipline is indeed a divine mandate that a parent must provide for their children (Proverbs 13:24, 19:18, 22:6, 15, 23:13-14, 29:15, 17), with fear and trembling, but not condemnation (Ephesians 6:1-4, Colossians 3:20-21—note especially the concerns about fathers being overbearing and harsh). Just as the Lord pursues and corrects us gently, faithfully, and with great love, so we should discipline our children. What the Bible defines as discipline, such as with a "rod" should not be perverted into physical abuse. And neither should exhortation to our children be communicated in a way that conveys anger or condemnation. Consider that physical abuse is evil and often very noticeable in the forms of visible bruises and scars, but emotional abuse is just as evil and often yields harder to discern bruises and scars in the heart of our dear children. Does God ever hate us? Does he seek to remove us from his presence until his anger abates? Does he castigate us, scold us, or reproach us? Are you struggling with answering these questions? If so, perhaps you also struggle in your parenting of your children.

Meanwhile, there seems to be a growing movement to say that all physical punishment via the rod is *de facto*, inherently abusive. This notion too, I think, perpetuates a great evil. Children need boundaries, and until they possess a greater capacity to reason and process good and evil, the physical stimulus of a spanking is useful to keep them safe. Children should know that they should immediately obey their parents—it is for their good. Discipline should happen quickly and persistently, but only once it is clear that children understand that they are disobeying, and only for disobeying. Being clumsy or easily distracted is not willful disobedience; it is simply being a child. My observation as a parent is that often, parents seek to be gentle with children, and thus do not discipline as they should, which in turn leads to pleading with and trying to cajole their children, which in turn can lead to exhaustion, exasperation, and anger. Everyone loses with this. Children never see the loving boundaries—boundaries that keep them safe—and so in their hearts, they feel abandoned. If there is a righteous God who loves us and pursues us, children first understand this God as they see that their parents are quick to lovingly discipline them and mentor them. Physical discipline, in turn, should be done with much love and grace. Parents should explain that they too struggle to obey the Lord, and that they love their children too much to let them disobey, and in fact are disciplining them out of obedience to God as well. And when spankings occur, they should be limited—a couple of swats—and afterwards, the hugging and cuddling should be far greater.

I have found that being persistent with discipline, but not overly harsh with the length or severity of spankings, when done at an early age, leads to very little spankings after the age of four. That is just my experience, but it also comes in the context of a lot of apologies from me when I lose my temper with my children. I often ask them whether it is there fault that daddy is mad at them or just grumpy. The correct answer is always "no"—if daddy is angry, that is something he needs to work on with the Lord; his own anger is a reflection of how he has forgotten that he is no longer an orphan, driven by fear and manipulation. As my children have gotten older, I have shared more of my own frailties; I want them to see that their parents are not perfect. They are learning to obey us because we are trying to show them what it means to obey the Lord, and part of that journey is sharing our own struggles and victories. Again, sin is the enemy, and we are clinging to Christ together. This is my best effort at helping them pass into adulthood, where our relationship as brothers and sisters in Christ will only deepen.

There is no question that parenting can be done in a spirit of legalism, perfectionism, and condemnation, just as there is no question that parenting can be done in a spirit of pacification of sin, abdication, and lack of self-control, where children manipulate their parents and are indulged in their temper tantrums. Either extreme is extremely harmful to children and parents alike, and leaves children quite vulnerable to feeling unloved and abandoned. Again, as noted above, these are very difficult topics, and I share my perspectives such as I am able, based on my understanding of God's Word and my own successes and failures as a parent. If you are a parent, remember how much God loves you as His child. You have a unique moment to love your children—it truly is a fleeting time as all mothers and fathers know. Remember that when you feel inadequate or overwhelmed, that you are not alone. Your Father is here to guide you in your parenting and to nourish you with wisdom and strength, just as in all things. You are no longer a rebel-orphan-slave.

CHAPTER 3
Of Conflicts, Churches, and Covenants

The imagery and ideas of covenant can be sublime, almost too sublime—they conjure up notions of ethereal living not appropriate for mere mortals.[1] Sure, the Holy Trinity abides in perfect covenantal fellowship, but not so for us. So, it might be helpful to spend some time discussing the real-world challenges of living covenantally with one another in two particular areas: conflict resolution and church. The previous chapter already provided some discussion on the nature of conflict resolution, but it is being addressed here because how people, teams, organizations, and movements handle conflicts make all the difference in terms of whether or not healthy, covenantal relationships exist or not. Meanwhile, church life is will be discussed here because healthy church life should be a natural extension of living out the Gospel and living covenantally with one another, and yet, so often that is not the case. We will discuss some reasons why and how to remedy that.

When people are faithful to living out the Gospel and to covenant-keeping, all of these challenges can be resolved. It always takes time and much patience, but persistence is its own reward: the very act of persistence builds and strengthens the relationship. To that end, what follows will be some principles that will hopefully guide us in walking through conflict in a covenantal, Gospel-centered manner.

Peace-Breaking, Peace-Faking, and Peace-Making

Much of the framework and thoughts on conflict resolution in the previous chapter and now in this chapter derive from Ken Sande's seminal book on conflict resolution: *The Peacemaker*. In it, he outlines the two extremes of failed conflict resolution. These were alluded to above, but will also be mentioned here. In *peace-faking*, people avoid conflict, due to "fear of man" issues, apathy toward others, and/or a desire for self-comfort and pleasure. It does take work, after all, to resolve conflicts, sometimes much work. It can be much easier, as noted in the previous chapter, to withdraw and/or gossip with others.

---

[1] Much like my ability to wake up suddenly in class, raise my hand, and offer at least semi-intelligent thought to the professor. I don't think my friend and classmate ever forgave me for that ability. But that's a "you" problem, Rob.

The gossip, back-biting and slander, in turn cause their own problems and certainly violate Scripture.

Peace-faking provides the illusion of being the easy way out. It does indeed seem much easier to walk away from difficult situations rather than persist and persevere to reach shared understanding. But walking away often means failing to love our neighbors and failing to preserve the Body of Christ. And we are hurt as well, when we withdraw. Conflict resolution usually takes self-awareness and self-growth. It requires us to not insist that our own way of thinking is always 100% correct, and requires us to look at painful shortcomings in our own life. That can be difficult, to say the least. But it is also one of the most effective ways to grow in Christ as it often takes others to help us see our own issues. A life lived in solitary confinement may feel easier, and in many cases it is, but it comes at the expense of spiritual and emotional growth and relational vitality, both with others and even with Christ. We are either a slave to Christ, where we will find true life, or a slave to sin, where we think we have freedom but only end up in the chains of nihilism, narcissism, and addiction. We either die to ourselves so that we can die to sin and find new life in Christ, or we die to eternal life so that we can live a life of death and self-absorption.

The other extreme, *peace-breaking*, is the more overt manifestation of unhealthy conflict. This speaks of the aggressor, the hot-head, the emotionally manipulative, verbally abusive control addict who must be right and who will not consider other viewpoints. In these cases, the aggressor is too dysfunctional and predatory to even engage. But in other cases, people—acting like people—are stubborn, prideful, self-righteous, and morally certain that their position is correct. So they lash out and attack others, causing conflict.

In either extreme though, whether peace-faking or peace-breaking, fear is often a driving force. Because we do not act with faith in God's sovereignty, we are overcome with worry and striving when we are confronted with personality conflict, disagreements over vision, strategy or tactics, or conflicts about all manner and types of resources. So, in extreme cases, we either lash out or we run. But *peace-making* affords a different path where we no longer are controlled by fear and anger.

In the act of *peace-making*, we lovingly and humbly confront others directly, with clear, objective communication (objective as possible). We learn to ask a lot of questions to seek clarity, and not the type of passive-aggressive "questusations"—questions that merely accuse rather than seek the truth. We also engage in a healthy analysis of our own issues and blind spots, with much prayer, feedback from others, and guidance from the Holy Spirit. Doing this is what Christ spoke of when He commanded the Pharisees to get the log out of their own eyes first before seeking to correct others (Matthew 7:5). Healthy conflict resolution leads to honest and open-minded questions and comments, asked directly to the relevant person as opposed to accusations and concerns being shared with outsiders. It also requires that the person sharing the concern also be open to hearing concerns about themselves. This is true covenant-keeping and contributes to a life well-lived. If covenantal bonds are the ties that strain, they are also the bonds that bring life and health—the bonds that sing life's sweet refrain.

Some Helpful Tips for Conflict Resolution

Flowery language aside, conflicts are a normal and abundant part of life. If we cannot resolve conflict then we cannot live as the children of God. No matter our ability to exposit deep theological truths, no matter our ability to pontificate about living for eternity, no matter our talents for the creative arts in worshiping God, no matter how good your book on covenantal principles is . . . if we cannot actually love people, we are not children of God (1 John 4:7-8). So, the topic of conflict resolution is both a necessary one and by default, an imminently practical one. Following, then, are some guidelines to remember when walking through conflict.

We Are Almost Always Part of the Problem

Let me start with a personal note—in all the conflicts I have had the sad privilege of being a part of, over many years, with many different people, in many different contexts and situations, there has always been one unifying commonality: me. You can say the same for yourself: whether you were the victim or the aggressor, you were involved. That is not to say that we are always the cause of the conflicts, but it is worth remembering that to every conflict, we bring our own preconceptions, expectations, and personality peculiarities that alas, make things different for other people and undoubtedly contribute to the conflict. It is helpful to remember that so that we can be quicker to listen and to look at our own issues, and slower to accuse others.

Conflict Stems from Our Beloved, Wonderful Personality Traits

Left for other books and motivational speakers is an in-depth discussion of personality traits. There are any number of different ways to discuss and classify personality traits. It is worth learning these concepts, to be sure, provided we do not overlook Biblical truth in doing so. Often, personality classification schemes seem to only focus on the strengths of our unique personality attributes without acknowledging any weaknesses. Happily, being guided by Biblical truth, we understand the doctrine of sin and how every personality trait can and does manifest itself in sinful and damaging ways. In fact, because these sinful tendencies are especially pernicious precisely because they are inherent to and key aspects of our personality. Such is life. Yes, we are indeed fearfully and wonderfully made, precious in the eyes of our loving Father, and thus wonderfully unique, but because of sin, we are each mean, selfish, and fearful, each in our own uniquely personal ways.

Again, Scripture is clear on the pervasiveness of sin, on how it controls us and confounds us, but even Christians do not like to talk about this. There are no inspirational Christian calendars or greeting cards with passages such as Jeremiah 17:9 or Mark 7:21-23. One does not often see Romans Chapter 7 printed on Christian-themed posters, bumper stickers, or T-shirts. And it is a shame that we are so uncomfortable discussing sin. Perhaps we are wrapped up in the idolatry of "positive self-esteem" that is only useful if it positively directs us to the love of God that comes through repentance in Christ; otherwise is just further enslaves us in sin. Perhaps we fall prey to the misnomer, indeed the great lie, that talking about personal sin is akin to hating ourselves, but that is no more true than talking about having a sickness is self-hate. On the contrary, identifying our ailments—physical or spiritual—is part of healthy self-care and growth. And if the One who knows us the most, loves us the most, should we not also want to know our own hearts? Part of understanding the hold of sin on our lives is understanding how our unique personality configuration, coupled with our unique upbringing, contributes to our uniquely sinful disposition as well as our uniquely, God-glorifying potential.

Conflict Is Inevitable

And this is why conflict is inevitable, because we are inevitably, uniquely flawed people who will never fully grasp reality. Just as our unique personality traits give us a unique perspective on reality, it also blinds us to other equally important facets of life and situations. This is why living covenantally is so important, because we need the perspectives of others to sharpen and augment our own blind spots, just as they need our perspective. Remember that living covenantally requires mutual accountability and care, principles that help everyone appreciate and submit to the perspectives of others. It also requires healthy vulnerability, of course, which in turn engenders healthy communication and conflict resolution and tends to limit fear and defensiveness. Meanwhile, the temptation can be to leave relationships whenever conflicts arise, as if conflicts could or should be avoided. Besides being unsustainable, this attitude is also detrimental to our own spiritual and emotional health and growth. The better approach is to expect conflicts and to know how to handle them. Leaving because of conflict only means that there will only be temporary relationships, because every relationship will ultimately fall into conflict.

Beware the Dangers of Unmet, Unspoken Expectations

When my wife and I were first engaged and participating in premarital counseling, our counselor, a stern but loving mentor with bushy eyebrows and scads of personality diagnostics, warned that "expectations are accidents waiting to happen." He explained this happy thought further by pointing out that both my fiancé and I would bring expectations to how married life should be due to our unique personalities and how we were raised. This would be problematic enough, but it would be even more difficult because most of the time, we would not even know we had them, until one of those expectations would not be met allowing for the possibility of hurt and anger.

The married folk reading this chapter can probably relate to experiences in their own marriages where this occurred, especially early on. My wife and I were grateful for being given a heads-up as this advice probably saved us from a lot of conflict. But it is a good piece of advice for any type of relationship. We often become offended at others because they did not live up to our expectations, which we never explicitly communicated, because we did not know we even had them. Humility and self-awareness, along with knowing not to idolize these expectations can go a long way toward avoiding unhealthy conflict. Further, gracious communication can help everyone voice their expectations and engage in covenant building to see how these expectations can be balanced, maintained, and fulfilled.

Conflict Can Be an Opportunity to Grow

In fact, conflict resolution is a wonderful important way to grow in wisdom, compassion, and healing. If we could be freed of the sinful ways that we hurt others, if we could overcome our own intellectual and emotional blind spots, and if we can help others do the same, why would we want anything but healthy conflict resolution as part of our daily relationships with others? But this takes patience, forbearance, and love. And above all, it takes faith in God, that He is guiding us in the process, because truly effective conflict resolution can take time, vulnerability, and trust.

It takes time because we do not easily or quickly disavow our own personality-driven perceptions. It rarely occurs to us that how we remember event and circumstances be driven by our personality framework or that another person's perceptions are important too. It is hard for us to understand that often, these different perspectives are not mutually exclusive, *but rather must be balanced and held in constant tension*, which, in fact, is possible in healthy relationships where frequent and engaged communication is the norm. It requires vulnerability to be honest with others about our flaws in a healthy way. If we are unhealthy in our vulnerability, we become easy prey for manipulative, abusive individuals who will use our weaknesses against us. On the other hand, if we are not vulnerable at all, we will never even consider the possibility that we might be wrong and we will never be able to have healthy, open conversations with others.

And in conclusion, this is why trust is needed—trust in God first, so that we can trust others. An orphan trusts no one; a rebel manipulates others and destroys trust, and a slave is incapable of the healthy self-autonomy needed for trust and thus often falls prey to the manipulation of others. A person who has found their trust and hope in Christ can then meaningfully and wisely trust others.

Church Life and Conflict

I write this section as a person raised in the church and who has devoted years of ministry therein, including serving in the capacity of small group leadership and an elder. I have had to endure the full gamut of conflict in the churches, from interpersonal conflict to large scale church divisions. It has all been hard, and only God knows the full extent to which I have perpetuated the problems. Church is supposed to afford us a place of safety, intimacy, vision, and growth. After all, our local church is an outpost of the kingdom of God, against which the gates of Hell shall not prevail (Matthew 16:18). No wonder then that conflict in churches can be so dispiriting and can engender so much cynicism and burnout. No wonder then that so many people leave the church over conflict.

And yet, the very reason that the church is so important and meaningful is the reason conflict can be so prevalent. We bring to church all of our expectations for heaven on earth. We expect relationships to be uniquely profound, we expect our own personal ministry gifts to be recognized, developed, and employed, and we expect church leaders to be uniquely set apart with integrity, maturity, and vision. As an aside, I suppose we do the same for our especially intimate relationships with others, like marriage, but when those relationships struggle or fail, we often hope that our local church can be a part of the solution to those flawed relationships.

But find a church with people in it, including leadership, and you will find a church with all of the normal problems that normal human beings have, including conflict. All of the factors discussed above that contribute to conflict are no less at work in the church, and in fact, can be even more prevalent because the stakes are so high for its members. We are easily undone when our sense of what the church should be is undermined by others in the church, whether through actual malice, differing perspectives about the vision and ministry, and just run of the mill human frailty.

It is for all of these reasons that we are easily disillusioned by conflict in our churches, but as an elder, I urge you to consider this—do not run from conflict in the church. Be a faithful witness to God's love and the power of the Gospel and press in when conflict arises to be a part of the solution and God's work. To do so, below are some helpful tips.

Do Not Idolize Church Leadership

Part of the reason we join a local church is because we are enamored with the vision, preaching, and ministry of the pastoral team and leaders. It can be easy to put them on a pedestal and assume that they are uniquely mature and blessed. But truly loving someone is not needing them to be superhuman and also requires knowing them well enough to recognize their tragic, imminently human flaws, and frailty. Church leaders also fall prey to the curse of sin. We hope that they are indeed mature in the Lord; indeed, they should be, but maturity does not equal perfection. Too often ministers cannot be real about their own struggles and burdens because church members have these unrealistic expectations. Thus, pastors try to bear the burden of ministry alone or possibly with few friends in the churches in which they are serving. This is so tragic, and likely accounts for why so many grow weary and eventually leave the ministry altogether (no doubt aided by gossip from the very members they are serving). Of course, truly loving your church's pastors and leaders also requires lovingly confronting them as needed, and thus means staying engaged in conflict in a thoughtful, loving, and Christ-centered way as discussed above and in Chapter 2.

Limit Your Involvement: Avoid Gossip and Slander

This loving, Christ-centered way means lovingly but firmly redirecting people who would gossip to you about church conflict back to the person with whom they disagree. In accordance with Matthew 18:15-20, the only time we should be discussing a conflict is when we are a direct party to the conflict or if someone is asking us to get involved. But our involvement should only come after that person has demonstrated that they have in fact tried to bring peace and reconciliation with the other party. If this has not happened, and the person is talking about the person or the situation with others, then that is simply gossip and slander.

Should it become necessary to become involved, again, only engage as a minister of reconciliation in accordance with 2 Corinthians 5:17-20. Kindly note that this engagement and ministry are as *ambassadors* for Christ. There are times when we must make a judgment of people's actions (1 Corinthians 5:11-6:11), but we should not sit in the seat of the scornful or engage in cynical, fear-based, speculative commentary about people or situations (Psalm 1:1-3). Remember how much the Enemy loves to fuel the flames of fear and anger-based speculation.

Perfect Conflict Resolution Will Not Happen This Side of Heaven

Instead of fear and anger, seek others out, in the ministry of reconciliation, to engage in thoughtful dialogue. As noted numerous times already, it must be stated again that it can take a lot of time to truly understand the perspective of others. This is true for both the leaders and the followers (in a variety of contexts). And often, despite the best of intentions along with thoughtful, loving communication, people still disagree. I wish it were not so, because it is far easier for people to grow discouraged owing to a failure to truly understand one another, much less agree. Often debates and discussions consist of repeating one's position, and often misstating or assuming the worst of the other person's position, with no allowance for the best-case scenarios or meaningful attempts to assume the best of others, rather than the worst. When this plays out in a church context, of course, the body is hurt—people withdraw, leave their local church, and perhaps leave the church altogether. It ought not be.

Do Not Idolize Your Vision for Ministry

For some specific organizational and church contexts, consider too that sometimes by virtue of a leader (and a leadership team's) unique gifts and callings, that they are in turn uniquely gifted to carry out a particular vision and ministry for the church. But this will often mean, by default, they will not be as gifted to carry out other equally valuable ministry ideas and opportunities that are important to other members of the church. This can lead to disappointment and even bitterness. As in all things, disagreements over ministry and vision can of course lead to conflict, and of course any conflict in the church between leaders and members should be clothed in humility and mutual submission (1 Peter 5:1-7). It takes humility for leaders to listen and embrace ideas that may fall outside what comes naturally to them, and it takes humility for members to recognize that no church can do everything. And as 1 Peter 5:7 reminds us, we should not be overcome with fear and anxiety, which are often the key driving forces of unhealthy conflict in churches (and everywhere else).

On the other hand, ideally, part of any church operation is the sense of covenant, specifically noncentralization, where members are empowered (and held accountable) to do the work of ministry in the church. Ideally, leaders and elders are eager to accept the ministry ideas of members provided that the members themselves are also empowered to lead and carry out that ministry. A church should not rely solely on ministers alone to do the ministry; after all, we are all ministers of the Gospel. But for this to be true, gentle reader, members have to be willing to actually *implement* the vision and not merely *suggest* the vision.

Conflict Resolution Prevents Evil

A final point is warranted about conflict resolution, particularly as it relates to church life. Elders and members alike are called to be wary of the wolves in sheep's clothing who seek to stir up trouble in the church (Matthew 7:15, Romans 16:17-18, 2 Corinthians 11:13-15, 2 Peter 2:1). This could be through immoral behavior inconsistent with the life of a child of God, or explicitly through gossip, slander, and political manipulations against church leadership. Sadly such behavior, of course, can be perpetuated by the church leadership itself. Further, in a more specific and direct area, too often churches have not properly addressed behaviors such as sexual and physical abuse, much less emotional abuse. In all of these cases, church leadership is mandated by God to exercise church discipline in accordance with Matthew 18:15-20, in order to protect the peace and purity of the church.

In the case of actual criminal behavior as noted above, this would also involve reporting such behavior to the local authorities. Just because such behavior happened in the church does *not* mean it is solely a church issue, no more than murder or other heinous crimes would be solely church issues simply because it happened in the pews. In short, evil must be addressed head-on. True, we must not be quick to jump to conclusions—we must be slow to speak and quick to listen (James 1:19)—but we must not be passive or fearful when confronting evil. If we do, we are failing to love our neighbor and failing to cherish and protect the bride of Christ. Countless hearts have been broken by a failure on the part of the people of God to properly address conflict and evil when they should have been addressed.

Conclusion

A final reminder: church life will disappoint you, because it is full of humans. You and I are just as much a part of the problem of church life as we are when we drive in heavy traffic—our presence adds to the problem. It is helpful to remember that, and that this is the very reason Christ came to die for us and save us. We persist in church life because Christ persists in his pursuit of us. Meanwhile, there is of course much more that could be said about conflict resolution and its place in the body of Christ. And just as easily, books upon books can and have been written on church life and vitality. On the latter, the next chapter focuses on general organizational life and leadership from a covenantal perspective, and so it will provide some further thoughts about what it means to live and act covenantally as leaders, followers, teams, and local churches. On the former, hopefully, the brief discussion in this chapter will encourage you to not run from conflict (nor charge into it!). Conflict is ordained by God, which is to say it is under His sovereign control. It is ordained by God because our free will is also allowed and ordained by God. We are people who even at the best of times trample and step on one another. We misunderstand one another, and try to accomplish tasks and goals in ways that often run contrary to how others would accomplish those same things. And that is if we even agree on what the goals and tasks should be, which we know is not always the case. Often we do not even define or understand the nature of problems in the same way, much less solutions.

Nevertheless, He desires us to seek and convey peace, to resolve conflicts in a manner which glorify Him, edify His Church, and contributes to our personal growth and sanctification. Moreover, conflict resolution, if done well, helps us to better understand and love the people God has placed in our lives, whether it be marriage, family, the church, or relationships in general. The process is not easy, and often is time-consuming, but most important things in life are the same.

When conflicts come—and they will—we can run or we can rage, but neither produce the godly fruit and eternal inheritance promised to us when we live as children of God. The common theme of this book still holds—rebel-orphan-slaves will always be victims of conflict—whether through their own deep and abiding anger and fear, or due to being trampled on by others of the same disposition (and often both). But being a child of the King affords a divine royalty that is more than just a position or title—it is a disposition and strength of heart (2 Timothy 1:7), fueled by God's unconditional love and acceptance in Christ—that allows us to wisely navigate conflicts, love others, and also address wrongs which do in fact need to be addressed in winsome, yet firm ways. So while it may be easier to just disengage when conflict arises, just remember that the other people involved in the conflict are former rebel-orphan-slaves, trying to find their way, by God's grace. Have mercy on them if they act irrationally. Forgive them when they are rude and thoughtless, for you will need their forgiveness as well, no less a former slave yourself (Colossians 3:12-14; Titus 3:3-6).

PART II:
Organizational and Political Applications

I opened the book with a brief recounting of my struggles to stay awake in class. Just to be clear, I worked hard and took my studies seriously. I just felt the need to offer that official statement, because this next section of the book is more academic in nature. This could be similarly off-putting or exciting, depending upon your disposition (and hopefully, there will be no rubber-necking for you, gentle reader). In either case, a few guiding thoughts might be helpful. When discussing the realms of professional, economic, and political behavior, as we will do in the coming chapters, one will, of course, have to employ technical terms and ideas. These are fine and useful in their proper place, but in terms of bringing the life and warmth our hearts so desperately need, they are inadequate substitutes, even tragically so, *particularly because we put so much hope in these things rather than in the Gospel.*

Ours is a dark and dying world, with the so-called experts being blind, and therefore have no hope of leading the rest of us who are also blind. But now, the Light has come (John 1:5), and we need not stay out in the dark and cold. We can bring these ideas of business and statecraft into the light of the Gospel and see how biblical, covenantal truths can inform those ideas and ensure they have life. Thus, they are important, and we should know them and understand their value. However, we should also remember that without the Gospel breathing life into these ideas, they are mere trinkets. And is not the history of mankind marked with emulations of trinkets to that of false gods?

To the extent that you have put your hope in these "trinkets"—these gold-plated metal images of academia, elitism, perfectionism, and professionalism—I hope that after reading the ideas here in their proper perspective, you might be convicted and freed from these wretched idols. I hope that as you put your hope more fully in Christ, as we all must do for the rest of our lives, you will, as Isaiah prophesies, "defile your carved idols overlaid with silver and your gold-plated metal images . . . " that you "will scatter them as unclean things. You will say to them, 'Be gone!'" (Psalms 33:20-22, ESV).

On the other hand, I also hope that in reading the following chapters, your love and enthusiasm for learning and wisdom will only increase. God is the Lord of all Wisdom, and Christ himself came to us as the Divine *Logos* (John 1:1-5). Willful ignorance and sloth are their own idols, ones easily and quickly purchased by fools. In contrast, you have before you a whole realm of professional, academic, and political experiences that have been gifted to us by God—whole fields of knowledge and inquiry, which we should see as our birthright—our divine gift—for we are indeed made in God's image. Therefore, love learning, love the big ideas, and love how the emanations, discussions, debates, and discoveries of science, theology, philosophy, economics, and business—all of it!—can lead you to even more joyfully love and worship your Lord and Savior, just as He loves and delights in you.

In conclusion, ignorance has two easy means of entrapping us. The first is indeed apathy and laziness fueled by arrogance, love of pleasure and ease, and self-importance: "the sluggard is wiser in his own eyes than seven men who can answer sensibly" (Proverbs 26:16, ESV). The other means is perhaps more duplicitous. It leads us through the path of academic learning and prestige to shed our fear and worship of the Lord, to set ourselves up as the source of wisdom, rather than God. This too, of course, is arrogant and leads us to ignorance, because we are too busy being scornful and insulting people with whom we disagree than to truly listen and check our own biases. Fools and scholars alike then, are just as easily entrapped by this beast; in either case, arrogance and ignorance are merely two sides of the same coin. As I have labored over the following chapters, my prayer is that the words I have written will allow you to hear the songs of creation, sung by wisdom. Its words are the call of the Father to embrace the joy of knowing Him, for his Son is indeed the Way, the Truth, and the Life (John 14:6).

CHAPTER 4
Interpersonal Dimensions of Organizational Leadership

An Unhappy Personal Note

I thought, as the beloved and well-intentioned author of this book, that I would share a bit about my personal education and background as we embark on a covenantal-biblical perspective on leadership. I have a PhD in organizational leadership with a major in government. I have researched and published on the biblical idea of covenant as a unifying theme for organizational leadership and behavior. It was in fact the major emphasis of my dissertation, which in turn led to several more published articles. However, as we all know, there is a significant difference between talking about leadership ideas and actually living out those ideas. It is one thing to talk about servant leadership; it is another thing to realize that in the midst of a busy schedule with a full inbox, numerous tasks to push through, and overwhelming minutia, the person at your office door is the person who God, in that moment, has entrusted you to serve and care for. With that caveat, let us commence with an understanding of how the biblical idea of covenant can serve as a guiding theme for organizational leadership and behavioral best practices.

*****

The message of the Gospel will suffer no hype; as we grasp the implications of why and how Jesus Christ saved us, hype and pretense tend to shrivel away. And this is a good outcome—a marvelous and wonderful outcome, even—to be saved from the stench of self-absorption and hubris. This reminder is offered here because there are few fields of inquiry that are so prone to hype and pretension as that of leadership. The world dreams of effective leadership. We cry for leaders to save us from corruption and evil. We long to have just the basics of competent leadership on the job—people who will let us do our job and treat us fairly. We aspire to be effective leaders and difference makers. And we also long to be the types of leaders who are celebrated for their virtue, inspiration, breadth and depth of wisdom, and impact.

And yet, the Gospel sees and preaches the truth of the matter: we are frail, vain, and easily undone by our own shortcomings, hardships, and vanity. It is easy to take credit for any success in life, ignoring God's grace, and blame God and others for the hardships and personal weaknesses we have, if we even admit them at all. Calvin said our hearts were idol factories, and there is nothing quite like the idol of leadership to confuse and distract from Christ. On the other hand, with Jesus Christ as our guide, we learn as fellow sojourners to cling to Christ together. When we do that, we can accomplish great and eternal things. How we lead and care for one another can and should be a part of this, and that involves not just personal leadership, but organizational leadership of churches, non-profits, businesses, and government.

This chapter certainly provides an overview of some of the key traits of effective leaders, but it will also hopefully dispense with the idols of leadership while also focusing on how a healthy organization behaves. One of the idols of leadership is the "super leader"—the personality-driven leadership style that emulates the leader but does not lead to true sustainable organizational health. But true leadership is not just about one person; rather, it is about how a healthy team or organization functions from top to bottom, in terms of structure, process, and cultures. Find a leader who only has charisma and excites followers, and you will find a leader whose impact on the organization fades away after they depart. This book started with the premise that we start with essential Gospel truths for essential living. So, it is with understanding effective leadership. We will discuss the idols of the heart that often undermine true leadership, and discuss Gospel-centered solutions. Likewise, we will look at the biblical idea of covenant as means for understanding effective organizational leadership, processes, structure, and culture. But first, we need to actually define leadership and its key attributes and dimensions.

Leadership Basics

A Working Definition of Leadership

For our purposes, leadership will be defined as *the use of personal, God-given gifts to positively influence people and situations for God's glory, both in an interpersonal and organizational context, regardless of one's position.* God gifts people in different ways for different things. It is easy to make comparisons with those that seem more gifted, and to forget that we too have been adopted by a loving Father. A particular set of gifts, or what seems to be a greater collection of gifts, should not be seen as evidence that the Father loves that person more than others. He loves all of his children. Nor should we see our own gifts as an opportunity for pride in comparison to others, because after all, they are gifts. We never get the glory (1 Corinthians 4:7).

We should rejoice in seeing others use their gifts for God's glory because those gifts are beautiful and a small picture of God's beauty and glory. And when we refine and hone our own gifts, we should do so knowing that it was the Holy Spirit who gifted us and empowered us to grow in maturity, which in turn allows us to possess a godly joy in our own Spirit-guided growth. All of the glory belongs to Him, but He shares that glory with us. It is always sad to see humans revert back to the orphan-slave—one who greedily seeks to snatch the gifts from God as if he has to fight for any comfort in this world. But we often act that way, do we not?

In a world that values talents, accomplishment, and learning, we exchange God's glory for the imminently hollow approval of men. It will always leave us empty and striving for more.

Far more satisfying is to see the gifts that God has given us as an opportunity to know Him more and to discover how He uniquely delights in us. How has the Lord gifted you? Will you use those gifts for his glory, and be faithful wherever the Lord has put you to glorify Him by caring for others and pointing them to Christ? Will you seek to ensure that your obedience is real—and not just talk—and that you really are making a difference and being obedient to the Lord? Of course, we do not get to determine how the Lord will use us or what He will accomplish in us—duty is ours, and results are God's. We just have to be obedient, and we have to be obedient in real and practical ways.

If we keep this in mind, we will be effective leaders regardless of where He places us or how He uses us. As this chapter proceeds, we will shift the discussion of leadership to more of those practical, organizational aspects. The Lord may have you in a formal position of power now or in the future. If so, this chapter will hopefully help you become better prepared for that, and it will also hopefully prepare you for being an effective leader regardless of what position you are in. Regardless, it is hoped that in reading this, you are encouraged to see that God has indeed gifted you and is preparing you for further leadership. It is entirely appropriate to rejoice in your unique gifts from the Lord, but moreover to rejoice *with* the Lord in those gifts, just as you celebrate the unique gifts of others.

Leadership vs. Management

Another foundational discussion in the field of organizational leadership is whether leadership is different from management. Many people argue that leadership is different from management because leadership focuses on casting and communicating vision, grasping the big picture, and getting people excited about what needs to get done. The argument for management, on the other hand, is that it is focused primarily on making sure things get done correctly, measuring success, and making sure people do what they are supposed to do. Are these two functions different? Yes. Leadership asks, "what is the right thing?"—that is where communicating the vision comes in. On the other hand, management asks, "What is the right way to do things?"

But it is important to remember that leadership is no good if it does not lead to changes and behavior that help an organization or group accomplish its purpose. By default, this requires practical and consistent outcomes and impacts. If leaders just talk a lot but do not deliver, then what good is that message? That is where management comes in. Likewise, for managers to be really effective, they have to motivate people by showing them how what they are doing connects to the big picture and how the vision is fulfilled. So, in the end, for leaders to be effective, they need to think like managers at times—they need to see how their big picture ideas are going to impact every level and process of the organization. Likewise, for managers to be effective, they need to think like leaders—they need to get employees excited about the vision and how they can contribute to it. And frankly, it seems rare to find leaders who are not encumbered with a heavy load of management duties.

That being said, remember what happens when we idolize results and outcomes at the expense of trusting God. First, failure to trust God leads to fear, and fear leads to workaholism and a constant state of crisis where leaders and followers alike feel the constant need to perform, perform, perform. Any sense of rest and work-life balance is, for all practical purposes and outcomes, discarded, even if corporate policies pay lip service to it. This problem stems from one of the many idols of leadership, which will be discussed below. But before we discuss the idols of leadership—that is, the counterfeit of what could and should be—we should of course start with the real thing; that is, what it means to lead as a child of God.

Between God and Man: Imago Dei

Fearfully and Wonderfully Made—Personal Attributes of Leadership

By virtue of being made in God's image, we all have unique gifts. There are generally a set of recognizable attributes associated with leadership skills. Some fall more on personal attributes and characteristics; some in contrast are skills that can be developed. So, for instance, extraversion and charisma are personal attributes that are often recognized as effective leadership attributes, but effective public speaking is a skill that can be developed with practice, even for introverts. You may or may not possess the recognized attributes of leadership, but now that we understand leadership is more than just a formal position of leadership within an organization, but is also influence for good or bad, we realize that we can and should use the gifts God has given us, whatever they may be, to love and serve others. This attitude and behavior are the first step for effective leadership, and lay the foundation for a healthy organization.

Related to this is the understanding that moral behavior is something anyone can and should develop. Remember that throughout the book of Proverbs, righteous behavior is equated to wisdom (Chapter 1 is a good example of this). We demonstrate wisdom by growing in maturity in Christ. The moment that this growth in Christ becomes a source of pride is the moment it is no longer either Christ-centered or true moral growth. All it has become in that denigrated state is an act of self-sufficiency, pride, and ultimately, narcissism. This reminds us of the dangers of pride, in general, when we flaunt our natural gifts rather than use them for God's glory. As the apostle Paul reminded the very contentious church of Corinth, which had become plagued by petty and prideful rivalry:

> "For who sees anything different in you? What do you have that you did not receive? If then you received it, why do you boast as if you did not receive it?" (1 Corinthians 4:7)

Thus, as you seek to develop yourself as a leader, avoid the pitfall of pride; it is a foolish and nonsensical trap, for we did not create ourselves or assign ourselves unique personality gifts. They came from a sovereign Creator and through no credit to ourselves. Having said that, properly recognizing these gifts, not only in ourselves but also in others, becomes the basis for one of the most powerful and effective acts of leadership: empowerment.

The Nature of Empowerment

To explain this concept, we start with what we have emphasized before—that we are made in God's image and fearfully wonderfully made. If we are made in God's image, then we have a certain degree of skills, gifts, and abilities that should be recognized by others. Effective leadership recognizes and affirms this in followers. This is known as *empowerment*, and it is probably one of the more powerful and all-inclusive ideas as it relates to leadership. In every realm of best practices in the areas of organizational leadership, processes, structure, and culture (OLPSC) as identified by researchers and thought leaders, empowerment continues to manifest as an important concept. Later, we will explain that empowerment is a key facet of covenantal behavior, for covenantal engagement requires the currency of mutual respect, care, and accountability.

But in the meantime, consider what empowerment means in a leadership and organizational context. It means that leaders make space for the unique insights, skills, and contributions of others. It means that rather than being the center of attention, good leaders seek to find and develop the unique contributions of followers. However, empowerment is not simply the act of some munificent leader, deigning to bestow some lowly followers with some gift of empowerment; rather, true empowerment is the act of humans recognizing the *imago dei* in others. In other words, it already existed inherent to people and is not something bestowed upon them by leaders. Only foolish leaders fail to recognize this.

So, empowerment is a prerequisite to loving our neighbors as ourselves. Leaders who fail to recognize this are failing the most basic act of human dignity and love required by God toward others. And, in fact, to love God well is to love others; this is true empowerment. Therefore, when a leader empowers followers, what should really be happening is that the leader is simply recognizing the grace of God and the *imago dei* in others. The fear of God requires this; to do otherwise is to mock the Creator and to pretend that one appeared and evolved through his own volition.

So many of us simply want that this recognition and act of empowerment on the job—the space to be creative and the authority and resources to act on that creativity. We want to have a say in how organizational decisions impact our work routines and processes. To be encumbered by decisions, which do not comport with the realities of our work processes, realities and constraints can weigh heavily on followers and damage morale. So, this should be encouraging for aspiring leaders: it is easy to lead well by simply loving and respecting others on the job. This means, among other things, making time to ask questions. Leave space in the process of creating and implementing the vision for the insights of others. Doing so negates the possibility of having established your own vision, that is true—you will in fact have to share the act of vision creation with others. The question is, will you trust God in doing so? Will you trust that God has uniquely gifted others as well to create and contribute to a vision and the processes to implement and maintain it? And finally, was it ever really "your" vision to begin with, or are you just a steward of what God intends and of his vision?

In the field of leadership and organizational development, vision creation and casting can be lifted up as some magic, inspirational act of true leadership. Often leaders try to change the very course of an organization by changing the vision. These efforts often fail—one study suggested that most fail within six months of implementation. The reason offered for such failure is that the vision comes down from the top-down—from leaders to followers. Yes, followers will try to march in step with such a vision, but the busyness of organizational life and perhaps the very fact that leaders created the vision alone without meaningful input from followers doom the vision.

Further, in the end, having a "transformative vision" might be a bit of idolatry in and of itself. What does an organization need to thrive? People need to feel cared for and respected. Their work and craftsmanship, specifically as it impacts customers, need to be valued. Does this require a uniquely transformative vision? Perhaps, but not at the expense of basic human decency and empowerment. Love others, respect them, and make sure that everyone, as much as possible, does the same. Yes, sometimes the most important act of leadership is removing the trouble causers who do not care about others. Thus, the first step of effective leadership might be as simple as empowering others.

Sin and the Problem of Selfish Empowerment

While the act of empowering others is a simple truth to understand, it is perilously difficult to walk out as a leader. All of us want to be empowered; we chafe under the heavy weight of arbitrary and thoughtless leadership. But when we are given some modicum of empowerment, we often hoard it selfishly. We resist efforts to involve other team members or departments in the creation of vision, policies, and programs. After all, we have finally risen the ranks so that we do get to have some decision-making ability. Why then would we share it? The reasons for doing so have all been mentioned above; this section exists just merely to gently acknowledge that it can be difficult to walk out. There is nothing worse than killing lofty and glorious ideals through selfishness and a lack of faith in God.

Servant Leadership and Following Christ

And yes, failing to love and empower others certainly demonstrates a lack of faith. As Christians, we have the opportunity to live for eternity—we are no longer rebel orphan-slaves. Yes, we must surrender our own agenda, but in Christ, we finally recognize that we should never have trusted our own perceptions of reality and what should happen; instead, we surrender to God. So, part of leading well, as an act of empowering others, is serving them and making sure they have the resources to succeed. There is an entire field devoted to the topic of servant leadership, and yes, again, it can be quite lofty and flowery in its exposition. It can also co-opt the Gospel by reducing Christ to merely a good example of a true servant, rather than fully proclaiming Him as the Savior of the world, the Lord of all creation, the King of Kings, and the faithful High Priest who alone can conquer and free us from sin.

To the extent that we can remember that Christ alone can free us from sin, we can effectively serve others and practice servant leadership on the job, in ministry, and in relationships with others. This is the act of losing our lives so that we might find it in Christ. This is a noble ideal, but it also has practical outworking for how we resolve conflicts with others, how we make time to listen to others and encourage them, and how we rearrange our own priorities and goals to accommodate the goals and priorities of others. In an organizational context, we can see how powerful this is, and how it can truly contribute to long-lasting and healthy organizations among everyone on the team. Hierarchy and power are de-emphasized; mutual care and accountability are instead lifted up.

Transformational Leadership and Covenant Keeping

From there, we can tackle another popular idea of leadership known as transformational leadership. This type of leadership involves creating an inspiring vision, exciting others with that vision, and recognizing the unique gifts that followers have to carry out the vision. Again, there is always the potential for hype and hyperbole with this idea. In fact, within the professional context, the term *transformational* is perhaps one of the most over-used terms (at least from my perspective and experience)—it has the scent of pixie dust and unicorns about it. But in its proper context, where leaders do not anoint themselves as some sort of priestly class of anointed vision-keepers, this idea has a lot of merit.

First, leaders are in fact charged with protecting the vision. Noting the concerns about vision implementation as discussed previously, leaders certainly must do a good job of reminding everyone on the team about the higher ideas of what it means to be humans, made in God's image, working together. This sounds like an easy task, and would be, if this is all leaders had to accomplish. But they do not—none of us can simply focus on "vision-casting"; we all have management duties and busyness which can overwhelm us. Part of living for eternity and living by faith is making time to care for others. And yes, while the most important "vision" is loving God and loving others, every organization has its own unique vision and mission. Part of a leader's job is to make sure that everyone remembers that. Remember the discussion on leadership versus management—every effective leader has to be effective at both leading and managing, but too often it can be easy to let the press of this world and the busyness of the work reduce us merely to worker drones who must meet our quotas and our deadlines. Part of being a good leader is protecting everyone else from this tendency and affirming the *imago dei* of followers. Yes, this requires scheduling celebratory events just for people who can have fun and remember that they enjoy being a part of a team.

But it also requires recognizing that as a leader, your schedule is not your own. You may be a "Type A" personality who has a near-unending "To-Do" list. You might enjoy slaying those tasks on the list one after another. But again, it is not your list, and the good Lord delights in sending people and ministry opportunities along your path, which disrupts said list. Trust God with your daily schedule; slow down, and learn to abide in Christ. If not, you will be consumed by your tasks, and your team and organization will be consumed as a result. You set the tone, and to set it well, you must abide in Christ.

Authentic Leadership and the Cross of Christ

This notion of abiding in Christ, which is both our greatest joy as a Christian and also likely our most difficult task, relates to another popular leadership idea: authentic leadership. This approach emphasizes the "anti-hype" leader who simply cares for others, creates a productive workplace, and is faithful to keep their word and act with integrity and decency. In turn, there is a depth of influence and impact which comes when one person decides to be present for another seeking to find their way—to assist through the painful passages of life, and to make time for detailed and often complex conversations that come with a person trying to find their way and figure themselves out. Make no mistake—this type of mentoring and care is indeed a type of leadership, regardless of the position held, or in spite of there being no official position of leadership at all. There are countless numbers of kind-hearted people who have done this and have therefore qualified for a type of leadership that has eternal implications for the good of the person they are loving. You might be one of those kind-hearted people who need to be encouraged that your kindness toward others will have a lasting impact even if your place on the organizational chart does not stand out.

Idols of Leadership

Raging Control or Abdication

The previous section discussed the implications for personal leadership traits and styles when properly centered in the Gospel. In this section, we will examine what happens when we remove the Gospel emphasis. Several idols exist; the first of which is the idol of control or abdication. We have all heard stories of leaders on power trips, who care more about their own power and prestige than what is best for the organization, and on the other extreme, we are well acquainted with irresponsible and negligent leaders. Both are tragic and toxic for a healthy organization. Remember what happens with spiritual orphanhood and insecurity—either we will exploit others to give us a sense of control and security or we will withdraw and abdicate because we are afraid of staying engaged. This abdication is itself a false sense of security. Above, we talked about successful leadership being about wisdom, righteousness, and integrity. As you seek to develop your career and advance up the ladder, it will be a good idea to look at some of the sinful motives that come with wanting to be a leader.

The Promotion Fallacy

For instance, if we are seeking to be promoted over others as an end unto itself, it is probably because we want to be viewed as better than others. This runs directly contrary to identifying ourselves with Jesus Christ so that he, not us, gets all of the glory. If we "need" recognition, then minimally, perhaps we are focusing on outcomes rather than obedience. As Christians, we do not get to determine the outcomes of our hard work—we just have to obey God and make sure we are doing what we are supposed to do to honor Him. We also never want to put the approval of man—which comes through our own effort—with approval from God—which comes through God's grace in the person of Jesus Christ. If the approval of men becomes an idol, we will not practice wisdom and integrity, or we will do the "right things" for the wrong reasons. Likewise, if we find that we "must" be in control (as if that were just a personality quirk rather than a fundamental statement about how we view God's role in our lives) then, yet again, we are being wrongly motivated.

There is nothing wrong with wanting to show oneself to be faithful and worthy of being promoted. But it is a poor hook on which to hang one's hat. Consider the reality: if God's only definition of success is promotion, then most people will not be able to please God since there are less and less available positions within any organization. Only a few people can be promoted in the end. Is this really the best way to view one's success?

Discussing idols of leadership makes for a helpful review of the dangers of Christian perfectionism, legalism, and pride. Performance-based Christianity, which itself is a counterfeit of the Gospel of Jesus Christ and God's unfailing love and grace, emphasizes outward works and self-sufficiency instead of healthy, authentic relationships. Even doing good things as a leader, but in a self-sufficient, perfectionist manner, can create a culture that is work-based and driven by impression management and pride. When leaders succumb to perfectionism and pride, they make the act of leadership, which should be driven by covenant, instead an act of self-glorification and striving. This reproduces itself throughout the organization. People work harder and harder to achieve, and there is little time for work-life balance, appropriate rest and reflection, and relationship building.

There is a great cost to the leader who engages in this dysfunctional leadership approach. Leaders who idolize themselves can be put on a pedestal by followers, which leaves very little room for healthy vulnerability. They can find themselves overwhelmed by the idolatry itself, as it becomes a monster that cannot be tamed. Leaders can begin to justify their own sinful, toxic actions in the name of all the good they are doing, and often, in fact, they are doing genuinely good things. But sexual sins, financial mismanagement, and controlling, manipulative behaviors are just some of the signs of leadership idolatry, and of course, a person guilty of these actions is also quite far from home—far from the arms of a loving Father who would heal the wounds caused by sinful, perfectionist, addictive behaviors.

Avoiding Vision-Killers

If leaders really want to ensure a healthy, self-sustaining organization that is proactive in meeting the demands of ministry or a hyper-competitive global economy, they must be sure to avoid vision-killers. Vision-killers are ethical and moral lapses on the part of leaders. It need not be a huge lapse. Nevertheless, these vision killers spread through the organization's grapevine, and sooner rather than later, everyone knows about them. This causes resentment and cynicism toward the organization's stated mission, values, and big picture ideas. Leaders become construed as big talkers and hypocrites who are out of touch with employees—especially when those vision-killers are directed at employees in some form or another.

Measurement, Management, and Manipulation

A major vision killer is caused when organizations and leaders put more emphasis on profit and quantitative outcomes at the expense of respecting and caring for team members. Note again the comments about management and its importance to effective leadership; here, note the dangers of making management of tasks and measurement of success the primary goal of leadership. This can happen when leaders, abandoning their hope in Christ, seek to accomplish organizational goals—even ministry goals—in their own strength. This can create a thoughtless, ham-fisted culture that focuses on results and results only. It also seems to generate a top-down approach where leaders only want followers to report results, not contribute to a healthy dialogue of what those results should be, how best to achieve those results, and any pitfalls that might result. This type of culture treats team members as worker drones. To be sure, it is hard in larger organizations to engage everyone to make sure that results are not idolized, and certainly, it does to no team or organization any good if a culture of laziness and apathy permeate work and interaction. A balance must be achieved, and it takes a committed team of people to make sure that balance is realized.

The Idolatry of Wanting Results

And even if the leader knows to avoid these more overt forms of idolatry, there is always the temptation of idolizing results. After all, we want to know we are making a difference! If we make results the ultimate measure of our efforts, rather than resting in God's unconditional love as we seek to obey Him, we will fall prey to idolizing outcomes. This can lead to a perilous trap—a long and twisted path back into the thickets of idolatry, perfectionism, and the ways of the rebel orphan-slave yet again. Doing good things, for the wrong reasons and in the wrong ways, is indeed one of the most powerfully deceptive methods of our old slave-master.

A Worthy Leadership Goal

Then what should motivate us? Living for eternity—seeing God work through us to change lives around us. There are only three things that will last for eternity—God, His word, and people, so we should invest our time and effort into them. As Romans 2:6-8 (ESV) says:

> He will render to each one according to his works: to those who by patience in well-doing seek for glory and honor and immortality, he will give eternal life; but for those who are self-seeking and do not obey the truth, but obey unrighteousness, there will be wrath and fury.

CHAPTER 5
Leadership as Applied to Organizational Structure, Processes, and Culture

A Covenantal Emphasis on Organizational Leadership

Often, as noted above, conversations and lectures on leadership seem to only focus on the role of an individual inspiring and serving others to achieve great change. In turn, this is probably where there is the greatest hype and hubris, because the image of the "messiah leader" often seems to be on the fringes of such conversations. Meanwhile, aside from the grousing of your author who maybe has studied leadership theory too much and is perhaps a bit jaded, another concern with this perspective is simply that it over-emphasizes the impact of the individual leader at the expense of what it means to have a healthy organization in the following mutually important and overlapping areas: processes, structure, and culture. This book has certainly tried to emphasize the wisdom of valuing the individual life and work of every person, even when we are not in a position of formal leadership. Loving others and living for eternity can absolutely impact the direction and destiny of other people, organizations, and groups. So again, in keeping with the themes and emphases of this book, this chapter in particular focuses on organizational leadership, processes, structure, and culture (OLPSC) starting with the intrapersonal relationship between us and God and moving to the organizational context, where hopefully we can learn to live in covenant with one another. In turn, we will see that OLPSC best practices can be divided in, and more importantly, guided by, the following key covenantal ideas: *hesed*, mutual accountability, and noncentralization.

Hesed

There are three key terms associated with the notion of covenant and covenantal behavior. The first is the Hebrew term *hesed*, which, as we know, means "loving fulfillment of covenant obligation." In Scripture, love and duty are intertwined and it is related to what Christ said when He told His followers to "go the extra mile" in serving one another. We see in Scripture that not only did God keep His promises to His people, but He went above and beyond His stated duties in showing mercy, forgiving, and caring for His people, ultimately through the sacrifice of Jesus Christ. We are required to do the same. We should not view our relationships with others as merely contractual obligations, but rather we should see our obligations as opportunities to truly love and care for one another. The implications for this interlinking of love and duty in an organization are significant. We all know leaders who have abused their powers and treated employees poorly, and we all know employees who have done the bare minimum (or worse) to collect a paycheck.

Mutual Accountability

Mutual accountability describes the process of interaction in a covenant in which everyone is accountable to everyone else. Not only are followers accountable to leaders, but leaders are also accountable to followers. Regardless of the nature of the relationship, be it peer to peer or leader to subordinate, mutual accountability is a requirement. This is because no one enters into the covenantal agreement without first securing this obligation. Because no can be coerced into such a relationship, the only reason for doing so is to create a binding relationship that assures everyone's mutual benefit. An organization that applies this will have greater integrity, teamwork, and decision-making because everyone is committed to serving and caring for everyone else, and leaders, as a general rule, cannot act arbitrarily and in a manner that mistreats employees.

Federalism and Noncentralization

Federalism is a specific term in the field of covenantal theology that describes the sharing of power among all members of the covenant. It is therefore related to the notion of mutual accountability and is embodied on the organizational level by the ideas of empowerment, participatory decision-making and decentralization (or more accurately, noncentralization, which signifies a sense of teamwork and shared responsibility regardless of organizational structure and departmental guidelines).

Hesed in the Organizational Context: Culture and Communication

Communication among Leaders and Followers

Much can be said about communication strategies and tactics, word choices, and semantics. But the first step in effectively communicating is loving others enough to listen well and to respond thoughtfully. A clear test that this is not happening is when we are too busy formulating a response to what someone is saying while they are still talking. We humans do not like to listen well because listening well requires an acknowledgement that we do not know as much as we think we do, and that others might actually have useful insights and ideas. And yet, whether in conflict resolution, team-building, or vision-casting, so much of effective communication begins with solid, reflective listening. Reflective listening in turn allows us to better make the case for our own ideas and goals, since we better understand the perspective of others.

Loving well enough to listen well in turn positions us to lead well. We gain credibility by listening and acting on feedback from others. This is the process of consensus and covenant building. Remember that part of forming a covenant is harkening—choosing to listen. Will we choose to listen? Conflict resolution requires this as well. It is not often that people in disagreement see eye-to-eye on even the most basic disputes and those differences will never be overcome if we do not listen well and communicate our thoughts in ways that consider the concerns of others. Certainly, leaders can bully their way through a conflict, especially if they possess legitimate power. But in doing so, they will likely use referent power, which in turns constitutes a vision-killer.

And to be fair, followers must also learn to listen well. Doing so is part of protecting the relationships and covenant. Listening well is not the same thing as abdicating to abusive leadership or covering up wrongdoing; rather, if there are those types of behaviors, listening well helps ensure that all of the facts are collected. If those behaviors are not present, listening and communicating well prevents a lot of the gossip and slander, driven by anger and fear, which can and has destroyed many relationships.

Building a Shared Vision

Covenant-keeping communication leads to effective vision-building. We discussed above the dangers leaders face when idolizing their own ideas of what the vision should be. Naturally, we expect leaders to have a sense of vision. This ability to see the big picture, which we will call "big picture thinking" is often a vital skill, which not everyone possesses. Part of what makes a leader a leader is this very attribute. But having a sense of vision does not mean that only the leader should possess or create the vision. Far more covenantal and effective for avoiding the pitfalls and idolatry of leadership is for leaders to communicate with followers to increase everyone's big picture thinking. This takes time and it takes effective listening skills.

When leaders and followers interact, followers have a better sense of the big picture challenges and constraints the organization faces, but leaders also gain a better understanding of the challenges and constraints impeding team members from carrying out the organizational processes and goals. This healthy, covenantal interaction, driven by mutual care and concern, and *hesed* can help to clear up frustrations, misunderstandings, and fears, while also building momentum for a shared vision. Again, leaders who are task or results driven will not see this type of communication and vision-building as a useful task, but in fact, it is probably one of the most powerful forces for enhancing morale, which in turn creates a sense where everyone is willing to go the extra mile to accomplish the very tasks and goals leaders can be so concerned about.

Mutual Accountability and Organizational Processes

Decision-Making, Active Dialogue, and Big Picture Thinking

Covenant-keeping requires humility, because it also requires vulnerability and intimacy. Leaders and followers often fail to see eye-to-eye, and often brag or complain about how the other side is uniformed at best and aggressively stupid and evil at worst. But in a covenantal approach, leaders and followers alike learn to consistently communicate with each other. This is defined by the term *active dialogue*. The conversations are seen as an ongoing, permanent process, between leaders and followers, among teams and departments, and between the organization and external stakeholders. All of this is predicated upon the covenantal principle of mutual accountability; in a covenant, everyone is accountable one to another, across individual relationships, teams and departments, and hierarchical levels of organization. Yes, in the end, followers have to obey the mandates from leaders, but leaders do well to ensure that followers have a say, as much as possible, into the decisions that will impact them.

To do this well, then, leaders must plan time for feedback and engagement as much as possible. This is easier said than done, but then again, most of the important things in life usually are. Further, the time and cost it takes to ensure a good decision is made are far less than the time and cost taken to clean up a bad decision, to say nothing of the low morale among team members who are impacted by the bad decision. This process of active dialogue discussed above in turn leads to big picture thinking. Now, leaders and followers alike are able to see organizational constraints, goals, challenges, and opportunities. Often, big picture thinking in turn contributes to much excitement, because followers have taken ownership of their team and organization (because they have been empowered) and thus they are motivated to tackle new challenges and opportunities. The very process of working together to accomplish the vision becomes part of what makes the work so meaningful.

Performance Management

A related organizational process that should be fueled by mutual accountability is the process of performance management. After all, communicating expectations to employees and team members should be done in a spirit of *hesed* and mutual accountability. Followers should be clearly aware of expectations, and should have fair, objective feedback when leaders believe those expectations are not being met. If the organization has avoided idolizing results at the expense of relationships, the performance management process can be one that further develops employees and affirms commitment to organizational goals. But this also requires humility on the part of leaders, who must be open to counterpoints on the part of employees. In the end, after all, unfair performance management practices will only undermine morale.

On the other hand, leaders do indeed have a covenantal obligation to remove troublesome followers for the good of the team. While harsh leaders are often too quick to remove followers, apathetic and fearful leaders are too slow to do so, which only undermines the morale and resolve of the good, hard-working employees. So, in both respects—protecting the rights of followers who are in the performance review process and dealing with problematic employees who are not working hard and are causing strife—the process of performance management is indeed vitally important for maintaining the health of the covenant. Meanwhile, the performance review process should provide clear evidence of when objectives are not being met, based on an active dialogue with the employee. There should be no surprises coming into the performance review and really, a yearly performance review should not be the first time an employee is hearing about concerns.

On the front end of the process, leaders should consider allowing team members to hire their coworkers. By training and engaging the best workers on the team, who have a uniquely relevant perspective on the needs of the position, these employees can be a valuable resource in ensuring that the right types of new employees are hired. This in turn can avoid a lot of performance review problems before they ever start.

Noncentralization and Organizational Structure

Noncentralization vs. Decentralization

Noncentralization has been discussed as a key facet of a covenantal structure. Rather than denoting a "flatter" organizational hierarchy (decentralization), noncentralization reveals that the true power does not come first from the leadership team, but from the followers and team members within the organization. This is why ideas like servant leadership, transformational leadership, and authentic leadership, along with the key ideas of *hesed* and mutual accountability, are so important. And more to the point, noncentralization is a direct outworking of what happens when empowerment is practice in all facets of organizational life.

Boundaryless Communication

The notion of noncentralization in turn relates to the ideas such as "boundaryless organizations" and organic structures. Boundaryless organizations are those who realize that the boundaries between internal organizational processes and concerns and external consumers, communities, and needs are quite thin—everything overlaps and is interconnected. It also assumes that boundaries within the organization should not really be rigid since so many processes and tasks are interrelated. Thus, communication within and among all internal and external stakeholders should be robust, ongoing, and active. This perspective helps encourage creativity and productivity in a highly competitive, global marketplace, where today's organizations need to be able to adapt quickly.

Thoughts on a Covenantal Culture

Covenant, Empowerment, and Self-Sustaining Culture

In a covenant community, empowerment has been operationalized through *hesed* and mutual accountability. Clearly, all of these concepts are related to one another, and this division of covenantal principles into attitudes, processes, structures, and culture therefore allows for a lot of overlap. The goal of any organization and its leaders should be to create a self-sustaining, healthy culture where employees have taken ownership of organizational processes and goals and are working together to get things done and care for one another. The culture of a covenantal organization is again informed by *hesed*, which in turn contributes to a climate of mutual care and concern. A covenantal organization is one where members are part of a family and are valued. People work together to get the job done and also see themselves as part of their larger community. They care for the organization, and the organization cares for them. As can be seen, this covenantal perspective informs the entire domain of human relationships—first between God and man, then into the relationships we have with one another, into the organizational context and even at the national and international levels.

Further, a healthy organization is not just about one person; in contrast, it is full of engaged, empowered followers who have taken ownership of the vision and mission. This leads to a resiliency that becomes self-sustaining. It does not rely upon excessive rules and harsh punishments to coerce obedience; rather, it is fueled by the good will and covenantal behavior of everyone involved (or at least most people). Covenantal bonds can be broken by vision-killers, by an over-emphasis on outcomes at the expense of relationships, by leadership apathy or tyranny, by poorly resolved conflicts, and by self-absorption on the part of everyone involved. As these bonds are broken and disappear, the organization will find itself in a growing state of decay, and will no longer have this self-sustaining culture.

Thus, an organization's culture is a vital part of its success or failure. How people relate to one another, how people feel about their organization, its mission and vision, and the actions and words of leadership all comprise the culture of that company and can make or break the company. Organizational culture is hard to quantify, but because it is based on people's relationships with one another and their feelings about the organization, it is often viewed as more of a living, organic entity. Many of the topics in this chapter speak to this same sense—that leadership should be more about intuition, relationship, and authenticity than about hype, rules, or mere business activity.

Explaining Postmodernism

A big part of understanding the material in this section involves coming to terms with the notion of Postmodernism. Postmodernism as a worldview and perspective on life came into vogue in the second half of the 20th century. As the name suggests, it is meant to signify that we live in a time that has apparently moved on from the "Modern" Era. In turn, the Modern Era was based on *Modernism*, which evolved during the time of the enlightenment and the development of Secular Humanism.

Modernism basically argued that religious and spiritual beliefs were superstitious and outdated and that what mankind really needed was the use of logic, rationalism, science, and technology to solve all of its problems. Instead, the following things happened in the "Modern" Era, which eventually caused a rejection of Modernism in its many forms:

   a) The exploitation of indigenous peoples in other parts of the world due to the assumption that Western civilization was superior to other ways of life;
   b) The Industrial Revolution which many argued stifled human creativity and expression because of the factory/machine mindset it created;
   c) The use of science and technology to kill incredibly large numbers of people (in World Wars I and II and other wars);

d) The creation of "rational" states such as the former Soviet Union, which instead of being a modern utopia, brought tyranny, poverty, and torture and death of millions upon millions of people; and

e) Chauvinism and the devaluing of women.

All of these major failures of Modernism caused people in the West to begin to rethink how to live life. Sadly, rather than turning back to the God of the Bible, many people went to the other extreme and begin to talk about making sense of life in nonrational, mystical, and very personal ways. Absolute truth as a notion was rejected, since after all, it was nations who believed that their way was the only way to live who killed, enslaved, and went to war with others. In the Postmodern view of life, people are encouraged to make sense of life on their own terms, to do what works best for them regardless of any sense of absolute truth and morality, and to find "God" in a way that best makes sense to them. Often that view of God lends itself to a deification of nature and the cosmos, rather than an embrace of the Christian God, because the Christian God believes in absolute truth.

In terms of application in the workplace, ideas such as "spirituality in the workplace," "multiculturalism," and "feminism" have all sprung from the Postmodern viewpoint. Multiculturalism emphasizes that each cultural perspective is valuable and that organizations would do well to draw from these various cultural experiences by hiring people of diverse ethnic backgrounds (as opposed to just white men). Likewise, feminism argues that chauvinism has exploited women for too long and that it is time for women to have a place and a say in the workplace, as opposed to the way things were in the Modern Era, where women were relegated to the home and to child-rearing. The #MeToo and Black Lives Matter movements certainly are extensions of these concepts.

So, what does the Bible say about these concepts? For starters, Scripture does indeed affirm a position of absolute truth, and an absolute sense of right and wrong. This is a good thing because it means that there really are things such as love, justice, and beauty. Moreover, in a biblical, covenantal worldview, each individual has rights and unique contributions that can be offered. A belief in absolute truth need not hinder an appreciation of cultural diversity; in fact, cultures and people express the character of God in unique ways. From a covenantal perspective, these unique perspectives are valued. What is rejected, however, is a belief in moral and cultural relativism. There are values and truths that transcend cultural and personal boundaries. This is a good thing, for the reasons mentioned above. Organizations that are imbibed in a biblical worldview affirm both the rights and value of each organizational member, while at the same time upholding integrity and ethical values.

As for feminism, the Bible seems to affirm that men and women can lead in the workplace, even if it makes a distinction for only men serving as elders in church ministry. There are some who argue that male headship in the home and the church in turn requires men to lead all facets of society, but that seems to be a forced conclusion, especially when we remember that leadership first and foremost is about influence and occurs in the context and processes of mutual accountability.

Covenant and Spirituality in the Workplace

As noted above, *spirituality in the workplace* derives from the notion that humans are not just corporate slaves or machine parts—they could and should be able to find personal fulfillment on the job through the personal expression of work as well as in community and working with others. The Bible has much to say about this idea. Of course, true spirituality is linked to a personal relationship with God through Christ. In keeping with the Postmodern emphasis on mysticism and a rejection of absolute truth, popular notions of spirituality in the workplace do not affirm the centrality of Christ in all that we do. But for Christians, work is an expression of worship to God in which we use our unique gifts from God to serve Him and glorify Him. Work, therefore, is holy and must not be demeaned. It was a gift to Adam and Eve before the Fall, even (Genesis 1:28–31). Certainly, as leaders, we should never force employees to believe in Christ, but we can affirm our faith in Christ as we love them, encourage them, support them, and help them maximize their gifts through their work. All of this can occur within the context of a "spiritual" workplace.

But the biblical idea of covenant goes further in affirming spirituality in the workplace, insofar as we are called to live covenantally with one another and recognize that our actions and decisions affect those around us. We do not live in a vacuum. Biblically, the most important thing we can do is care for others as an act of worship and devotion to God. We cannot forget that. To some extent, the topic of acknowledging and caring for employees relates to the topic of spirituality in the workplace since there can be more than just doing of the task—there is a sense of community, mutual care, and teamwork.

In this community-based approach to spirituality in the workplace, everyone in the organization realizes that "we're all in this together" and that we should work hard to get things done with excellence and that we should care for one another. The act of "living well" and "doing well" perhaps become even greater than merely making a profit. The Bible calls us to love our neighbor and to live covenantally with one another. These biblical ideas are a solid foundation for what spirituality in the workplace should resemble. Finally, this sense of community and mutual care should go beyond the workplace—a healthy organization is going to involve collaborative partnerships with other stakeholders and community members.

Covenant as an Integrative Paradigm

In conclusion, note that the biblical idea of covenant can provide an integrative approach to leadership. *Hesed* describes the *attitude* that leaders should have with others in the context of interpersonal relationships. Mutual accountability describes the *processes* that leaders should set in place in organizations—practices such as empowerment, participative decision-making, active dialogue, and big picture thinking. To carry out those processes, leaders need to create *structures* based on ideas such as federalism and noncentralization, so that power can be shared among cross-functional teams, decentralized departments, and flatter communication networks. With structures in place, people will be better equipped to stay on the same page and communicate with one another. All of these things will hopefully lead to a *culture* that is self-sustaining—leaders and followers alike will embrace the ideas of big picture thinking, *hesed* and mutual accountability, and therefore take ownership of the processes and structures mentioned above.

This chapter has gone light on terminology related to OLPSC best practices. It was felt that the better route would be to focus on major themes rather than terms. But in the following table, the concepts in the left column do in fact represent some of the more popular terms and best practices associated with OLPSC. The rest of the columns break those best practices out into leadership, processes, structure, and culture. Finally, the bottom row reveals all of the related covenantal terms. Hopefully, this will be a good summary for how covenantal terms can be used to create an integrative paradigm or a healthy organization:

	LEADERSHIP BEHAVIOR	**PROCESSES**	**STRUCTURE**	**CULTURE**
Transformational Leadership	Vision-casting, empowering employees			
Servant Leadership	Serving, empowering employees			
Participative Decision-Making		Increased decision-making to employees		
Decentralization			Sharing power with employees	
Spirituality in the Workplace				Supportive, empowering atmosphere
Covenant	Empowerment (*hesed*)	Mutual accountability	Non-centralization	Mutual care and support (*hesed*)

In the next chapter, we will take these same biblical, covenantal concepts and apply them to the realm of government and statecraft.

CHAPTER 6
Personal Foundations of Justice and Society

Introduction

For over thirty years, in some form or fashion, I have been acquainted with the teaching and promulgation of what the Bible says about the role of the State. At the Christian high school I attended (where again, I mostly stayed awake, despite my classmates jokingly giving me, for some unknown reason, a plastic cover to protect my tie from drool . . . why would I ever need this?), I took a course entitled "Christian Self Government." The high quality, hard back book we used for the course is still sitting in one of my office bookshelves as I write this. After attending this Christian high school, I then attended Christian universities for all of my advanced degrees, from undergraduate to doctoral studies. Thus, I have been introduced to many thoughtful and intelligent ways of communicating these principles, at a depth not often taught from the church pulpit. I had the privilege of learning from theologians and legal scholars who provided in-depth analysis, often in the original Hebrew, Greek, and Latin of Scripture, of topics such as inalienable rights, covenant, and constitutionalism. Entire courses were devoted to these singular topics. (Older writers, might, at this point talk about how quickly time passes, and how they can remember that first high school class like it was yesterday. They would doubtless ruminate over the shortness of life and how we are all a vapor, and as they sit at their desk and look out their office window, take a moment to reflect that yes, thirty years is over half their life. But I will not do that here, because I am not old.)

In turn, after having been a student of these topics, readings, and coursework, I have developed my own curriculum and have taught extensively from those documents and ideas. In all of the material I have studied or developed myself, I have found that there is much overlap. There are many different ways to present these same concepts and they are all useful. In fact, because there is so much overlap among these principles, it can be hard to provide clearly drawn lines among them. Perhaps the better approach is to simply recognize when they overlap rather than forcing what doubtless would be arbitrary boundaries. In keeping with the overall approach of this book, what I would like to do in this chapter is to demonstrate how these principles derive from four basic areas or categories of thought:

The Character of God

- Justice
- Limited government

The Nature of Man

- Inalienable rights
- Sinfulness of man (and another reason for limited government)
- Covenant

The Relationship between Man and God

- Covenant
- The work of Christ: the separation of Church and State

Corporate Facets of Justice—Loving One's Neighbor (this will be discussed in chapter 7)

- Covenant, federalism, and noncentralization
- "Selfless" self-defense and resisting tyranny

Hopefully by now you have noticed that these same concepts have already been introduced and discussed in several of the previous chapters. That is because these same principles are at the core of who we are, and they continue to have application in the expanding, concentric circles of our interactions with one another, with our families, our churches, our organizations, and, as discussed in the coming chapters, our government and political activities. These categories are hopefully not just some arbitrary classifications, as they represent the basics of how God pursues us and covenants with us, and how we should in turn covenant with others. These ideas thus have very real and powerful implications for how a society should function. In each of these sections, there will be some discussion of public policy applications as well as some of the history of how these ideas have developed over the centuries. You will hopefully see the connection between how God made us and loves us to how Scripture would order society and government, in ways that maximize liberty, mutual accountability and care, and limit tyranny.

Having said that, abstract principles can seem a bit, well, abstract, in the press of current events and frenetic political activity. It is always easy to worry and fret about national and international developments, to feel helpless in the face of conspiracies, the machinations of power brokers, the fevered passions of people and their movements, and the economic, political, and military crises *du jour*. What are we mere mortals to do in the face of all of these things? The realm of statecraft and politics certainly calls for men and women of wisdom and integrity to step forth and make a difference, but even good people can be washed away in the tidal waves of processes, structures, and circumstances of the political arena.

Know this: while this chapter discusses key biblical ideas which can structure and reform government and politics, thereby hopefully equipping future statesmen and women, it will also provide the history of how those ideas have been implemented throughout history. So, we will see that what began as small ripples of change in Western Europe during the fall of Rome and then the rise of Medieval Europe, eventually took on enough power to wash upon the shores of a land which would one day be called the United States of America. Providing these concepts and events is not meant to venerate America as some sort of messiah nation. Rather, the hope is that the reader will be encouraged in understanding God's faithfulness in bringing about change, over centuries. We are not bound then, to the rise and fall of a political party or leader, or even a nation. God alone is the One who will not fail, and whose Purpose will be accomplished, always.

Understanding the historic progression of these ideas will also reveal God's incredible patience, which at first glance might not overwhelm the reader's heart with joy. We want quick change, quick relief from the evils and injustices of this world. We beg for God to intervene, to change society, to change *us*. Why is He seemingly so slow, so patient, in doing so? Let us go back to the beginning: the holy Trinity before time and space. Their beloved plan to create us in their own image required the gift of free will, which in turn required the presence of the Tree of the knowledge of good and evil, which lead to the Fall, which lead to tears, suffering and evils without number. But it also led to the God-Man walking this earth in time and space, choosing the Twelve, becoming our sacrifice and sending the Holy Spirit to empower the formerly confused and misguided disciples to begin the slow work of righting the world.

You see, it sometimes takes centuries for change to occur because God loves us. He gave us free will so that we might know the power and joy of choosing to do good and accepting God's love freely. Yes, even that choice requires God's divine unction and intervention; it is shrouded in the mystery of God's sovereignty which somehow also allows for our free will. But it is still our choice. And choices to love and fulfill the call of God cannot be made with coercion or manipulation. On a personal level, we know that choosing to step away from years of both personal and family history and habits and to begin a new path is a decision not easily made or practiced. If we were mere machines or robots, the good Lord could just give us a software upgrade and we would be fine; but because we are made in God's image and created to be loved and to love, the paths of change require a second-by-second abiding in the Vine. That is why God is so very patient with us and with his work at the level of society.

Nevertheless, it can be easy to find his patience distasteful, for it allows the accumulation of evil from one generation to the next and when that happens (and it always does), people suffer. It is understandable that many would ask how many hearts have been broken and bodies devoured by this patience, by the seeming unwillingness of God to quickly intervene and to judge the wicked. But the better question to ask is how many lives have been saved by this patience, over and over again? For if a truly righteous God were to truly enact true justice as quickly as we should receive it, we would all truly and instantly be damned. And eliminated. The slow passage of time and the passing down of evil and suffering from one generation to the next is evidence that the rainbow's promise still holds because rest assured, that passage of time also bears witness to the sovereign work of God—and his mercy—in our hearts and in society. From generation to generation, from one broken heart changed to a healed and whole child of God, from one society slowly reformed through revival and reform, we see that evil is not alone in the churning of time. God's grace is abundant and He is working, as sure as the Word of God became flesh and as sure as the Light entered the world and the darkness was not able to overcome it (John 1:5).

We do not revel in God's patience, love, or grace to overlook or ignore evil and the sufferings of others; on the contrary, we put our hope in God's patience, love and grace so that we might not grow weary as we seek to love our neighbor and to reform laws and structures so that the grind of evil might be overturned. We neither put our hope in government to end evil, nor do we withdraw from the political arena, for the same God who is patient is the One who gave us free will, and with free will comes the opportunity to choose, to take action, and to love our neighbors as ourselves. Some Christians decry political activity because it is inherently evil and sordid, and it will certainly stay that way if Christians do not become involved to reform it. Some Christians decry political activity because they fear the temptation of idolizing the State above God. This can certainly occur, but idolatry can occur with all things, even church life (sometimes especially church life), so the threat of idolatry is not enough of a reason either. Instead, we should seek political involvement as a means of worshiping God and living our lives for eternity. We engage politically because doing so allows us to love our neighbors as ourselves. It is certainly not the only way to do so, but it is one way, and it is an important way of doing so.

And so, we move the conversation forward with a very focused discussion of who we are in Christ and how we see ourselves in Christ. Make no mistake: who we are in our heart of hearts determines how we view the role of the State in all of the trials and challenges of our time. And who we are in our heart of hearts is determined by whether we believe, think, and act as sons and daughters of God or as rebels and orphans and slaves. We saw this in the previous section when leaders abandoned their adoption in Christ and inevitably exploit others or allow themselves to advocate their moral obligations as a leader. This deficit impacts not only interpersonal relationships but also the structure, process, and cultures of organization. This general pattern is true at the state level as well. People who fail to let the love of God fill their hearts will suffer from a desperate, spiritual insecurity. In turn, they will either exploit others or we allow themselves to be exploited; thereby abdicating their responsibilities, as discussed in the above example with the leader. This insecurity-exploitation pattern has been described in some detail in previous chapters but now we will look at how this problem impacts government, for who we are, in our heart of hearts, leads to whom we view as sovereign, and whom we view as sovereign leads to, as Burtness argues, either anarchy, tyranny, or liberty.[1]

A person who sees themselves as fully sovereign and autonomous without need for God's law or love will ultimately end up exploiting others. At a national level, this leads to anarchy, where everyone does "that which is right in their own eyes" and in the end, there is only rule by might, as the most powerful exploiters are able to control and manipulate others. This can

---

[1] Bill Burtness, *Judah Bible Curriculum: Education for Liberty* (Urbana, IL: Bill Burtness, 1991).

lead to a constant state of chaos and war, with unending blood feuds. But eventually, like nature abhors a vacuum, so people abhor anarchy—better to have brutal control than chaotic anarchy with roving bands of thugs and murderers. Incidentally, when a society is so afraid of the radicalism of Marxism, it can be easy in turn to look to a strong, authoritarian state to bring order. This is no better of an answer than the raging fires of radicalism, which only burns and does not build. Besides, tyranny itself often comes with roving bands of thugs and murderers, but it is differentiated from anarchy because tyranny is often the result of viewing the State, and not God, as sovereign. When the individual or the State are viewed as sovereign, there will always be a loss of liberty. When people reject God's law and love, there will always be a loss of liberty.

But when we allow God's love to remove that insecurity in our hearts, we are made whole, and worship no false gods, because a person who views God as sovereign learns to control his sin nature and to love others. We no longer crave unrestrained freedom, and so we are no longer bound by uncontrolled sin. We as Christians know this is true liberty (2 Corinthians 3:17-18), and we thank God for the saving work of Jesus Christ on the cross that made this liberty possible. We have found the "spring of water welling up to eternal life" from within, from Christ (John 4:14, ESV). Therefore, as we grow in power, love, and self-discipline rather than the fear and weakness (2 Timothy 1:7), we are no longer willing to have an arbitrary, tyrannical state controlling us. We do not need other people to tell us how to find fulfillment; we do not need someone else to provide for us; and we do not need anything from government but the protection from evildoers and injustice. Meanwhile, externally, to this government—a government that protects his freedom instead of stealing it—we willingly and respectfully submit.

	Who Is Sovereign?	
The Individual	**God**	The State
Anarchy	**Liberty/Self-government**	Tyranny

So, then what does a government predicated upon liberty and self-government resemble? We can answer this question by going back to the character of God and who He made us to be. An understanding of covenant will also help us understand how God has loved us and how in turn we must love others. God covenants with us because we are valuable. Yes, we are frail, prone to overreaction, manipulation, and fear. We bear the marks of sin, one and all. But one does not covenant with a sack of potatoes or a heap of dirt; we are inherently valuable and wonderful.

God's Character: Love and Justice, Natural Law, Church and State

Overview

Comprehending and appreciating God's character requires a glance back to the Calvary. We see that Christ fulfilled God's perfect love and justice on the cross. He balanced them and reconciled them so that neither were compromised and both were perfectly fulfilled. Any false religion that denies that Christ was fully God and fully man also denies this perfect fulfillment of love and justice. That the Father sent Jesus Christ, the God-man, the good-shepherd-become-sacrificial-lamb, the faithful and now risen High Priest, gives us a portrait of God's unchanging, uncompromising character, which requires both exact and complete justice and manifests unfailing, tender love.

Jesus Christ, as fully God and fully man, died on the cross for our sins. His sacrifice was the perfect legal remedy for the problem of sin. As fully God, Christ was perfect and sinless; as he stood before the righteous Judge on our behalf, he did not have to account for his own sin. He was indeed the perfect sacrifice. As fully man, he could in fact take on our punishment; the righteous law of God was still upheld. No rules were bent, no inherently eternal and righteous standards were ignored in God's efforts to save man. Therefore, all who put their hope in Christ by faith alone will be saved. But faith must be arrived at freely. It cannot be coerced. All those who are saved by grace in Christ will be also sanctified by grace in Christ. And above all, God is omniscient and all powerful, in case those were facts forgotten.

This begs for properly placed worship and enthusiasm—worship for God, and not for any human institution, specifically the State. Find people who believe that the State can be God by changing the heart of man and removing the scourge of evil, and you will find those who have idolized the State on a shabby alter built of bureaucratic red tape, judicial over-reach, and laws upon laws upon laws. At best this is a bureaucratic nightmare which even its least malignant form causes other realms of society like the Church and family to atrophy, and at worst effects a dark, thorough tyranny. This tyranny would seek a systematic expulsion of the roots of evil—human rights be damned—and yet is never able to root out the frailty and source of evil in the human heart. Even tyrants cannot ascend the throne of God.

Therefore, rather than trying to *be* God, government must always act within the authority prescribed to it *by* God. It follows, then, that God's Law is the source of man-made law. Emerging from the tradition of English common law and the Western legal tradition in general is the notion of "natural law"; that is, an inherent standard of right reason. Natural law is used to explain the presence of this standard of right and wrong. It most definitely comes from a biblical perspective as legal theorists such as William Blackstone explained that it coexisted with, but was subservient to, God's revealed law, that is, Scripture. Further, it was used in part to justify the existence of inalienable rights, which we will discuss below. But it is useful now to say that when the American founders spoke about the "pursuit of happiness" as an inherent right of each human, they were not speaking of some reckless pursuit of pleasure and ease; instead, they were speaking of the right to live one's life in accordance with God's will and his intended natural order.[2] This is the true liberty we spoke of above, involving self-government, freedom from the bondage of sin, but also submission to God, and a life lived well. In turn, because government is not the ultimate source of authority, it must be limited in nature.

God's sovereignty also places limitations on policy and law-making on the part of the State and political leaders, since justice does not originate from man-made law. Some argue

---

[2] Carli Conklin, *The Pursuit of Happiness in the Founding Era: An Intellectual History* (University of Missouri Press, 2019): 5–6.

that morals should change based on an evolving and consensual understanding of what is right and wrong: adhering to ancient, fixed standards of right and wrong, the argument goes, actually furthers repression of self-expression and freedom, and by default, encourages tyranny. However, this perspective provides no moral basis for signifying human beings as uniquely eligible for inalienable rights that cannot be infringed upon by the State or by society. If the State has the final say, then justice is malleable and can and will fall prey to those who have the most power. A sense of natural law, then, is a bulwark against such injustices because it presupposes God's authority and the State as subservient to that. Related to this notion of natural law is that of justice; in fact, it could be said that justice is the natural outworking of God's eternal, righteous law.

Justice

Therefore, it is no surprise that the Bible indeed has much to say about the notion of justice. Scripture affirms that just and fair dealings should be linked to every aspect of government—executive, legislative, and judicial, which includes prohibitions against perjury and slander.[3] This view of justice involves protecting the weak from the rich and powerful, as the prophets warn of impending doom on those who use their wealth to gain political influence via corruption and graft (Isaiah 10:1-2). But the Biblical view of justice goes further than that, warning that while the rich certainly exploit the poor, the real problem of evil is a personal, spiritual one. This is in contrast to a view of justice that solely focuses on external factors and economic processes (such as Marxism) or injustice that is inherent to the structure of society itself (such as distributive justice). A Biblical view of covenant further requires law enforcement agencies and personnel to be accountable to the people and to be meaningfully engaged with them.

The Hebrew term *mishpat* is an important Biblical term that links government activity with justice. *Mishpat*, which can be defined as "justice, ordinance, custom, or manner" represents what is

> doubtless the most important idea for correct understanding of government—whether of man by man or the whole creation of God. Though rendered "judgment" in most of the four hundred or so appearances of *mishpat* in the Hebrew Bible, this rendering is often defective for us moderns by reason of our novel way of distinctly separating legislative, executive, and judicial functions and functionaries in government. Hence *shapat*, the common verb (from which our word *mishpat* is derived) meaning "to rule, govern," referring to all functions of government is erroneously restricted to judicial processes only, whereas both the verb and noun include all these functions.[4]

---

[3] R. Laird Harris, Gleason L. Archer, Jr., and Bruce K. Watke, *Theological Wordbook of the Old Testament.* Volumes 1 & 2 (Chicago, IL: The Moody Press, 1980): 948.

[4] Harris, Gleason, and Archer, *Theological Workbook,* 948.

So, what government functions does the term *mishpat* entail? An analysis of the Bible reveals that there are thirteen separate yet interrelated government functions (defined by using the term *mishpat*), "which if to be rendered by a single English word with similar range of meaning, ought by all means to be the word 'justice.'"[5]

They are as follows:

1. The act of deciding a case of litigation brought before a civil magistrate...
2. The place of deciding a case of litigation...
3. The process of litigation...
4. A case of litigation (i.e., a specific cause brought to the magistrate)...
5. A sentence or decision issuing from a magistrate's court...
6. The time of judgment...
7. Sovereignty, the legal foundation of government in the sense of ultimate authority or right...
8. The attribute of justice in all correct personal civil administration is emphasized...
9. An ordinance of law—often used coordinately with *hoq* "ordinance" (Exodus 15:25) and *tora* "law" (Isaiah 42:4)...
10. A plan (Exodus 26:30) or
11. custom (2 Kings 17:33) or even
12. a fitting measure taken (I Kings 5:8) seem to come under the scope of this word...
13. One's right under law, human or divine, is denominated *mishpat* (Deuteronomy 18:3; Jeremiah 32:7).[6]

Justice, therefore, should be the basis of government. This is not merely a suggestion for government activity, it is a commandment: "When therefore the Scripture speaks of the *mishpat* of God, as it frequently does, the word has a particular shade of meaning and that is not so much just statutes of God as the *just claims* of God. 'God, who is the Lord, can demand and He does demand.' . . . Jehovah is the God of justice (Isaiah 30:18; cf. Genesis 18:25). God loves *mishpat* in this sense (Psalms 37:28)."[7]

This notion of justice stems directly from the character of God. The State must be just because God is just, and He requires it of His people. When the State abuses its power, violates the trust of the people, caters to the rich and powerful at the expense of the poor, the fatherless and the widow (Isaiah 10:1-2), when it is seduced with empire building rather than defense, when it appeals to and foments angry mobs rather than rule by law and justice, it defies the character and will of God. And finally, when it subverts the *imago dei* of its people, particularly by violating their inalienable rights, the State subverts justice. We will discuss the importance of inalienable rights in the next section.

---

[5] Ibid.

[6] Ibid., 948–9.

[7] Ibid., 949.

The Nature of Man: Inalienable Rights and Limited Government

The same beautiful, mysterious, all-powerful Triune Being, omniscient to the point of not only standing outside of the time-space continuum, but actually *creating* it, was the same entity that deigned to make us—to share his joy with us and to revel in the love and beauty of His joy with us. God the Father, God the Son, and God the Holy Spirit, three-in-one, gifted us with their *imago dei*. This royal designation is not and was not ever gender-specific—male and female were both made in God's image (Genesis 1:26; 9:6). We are staggered by the implications of this—to be given the opportunity to engage in covenant fellowship with God himself, without coercion, and to enjoy love and freedom for all of eternity. But in addition to all of the wonderful implications for our lives on an intrapersonal level and relationally with God, this *imago dei* notion leads to several interesting points of application for the role of the Church and the State.

Inalienable Rights

The first application is that if we are made in God's image, we are spiritual beings, designed to live under God's authority. By nature of being made in God's image, we possess inalienable rights. Inalienable rights are defined as those rights that are inherent to our personhood. They cannot be taken away, *nor can they be given away*. Inalienable rights are defined as life, liberty, and property as these three basic categories of rights are so basic and also necessary to living a meaningful and productive life. Without possession of these rights, we face the existential threats of essentially death and slavery. These rights are supported in Scripture; first by virtue of being made in God's image and by various commandments from the Old Testament (Genesis 1:26, 9:6, the Ten Commandments) as well as the most basic commandment affirmed in both the Old and New Testaments to love God and love others (Matthew 22:37-40).

In turn, government exists first and foremost to protect our inalienable rights and ensure justice. Citizens are required to participate in the political process as a means of limiting tyranny. Criminal and police investigations must protect inalienable rights. People must be assumed innocent until proven guilty, and undue force must be avoided in all processes. Any policies which violate the inalienable rights of human beings are unjust and should be opposed. The fact that we are made in the image of God, as Genesis 1:26 states, should remind us that no human should be disregarded as irrelevant or unworthy of protection. No government should dare to infringe upon the inalienable rights of any person, for to do so would be to disregard the very image of God. This truth is particularly relevant when we remember the words of Jesus Christ in Matthew 25:40 (ESV): "as you did it to one of the least of these my brothers, you did it to me."

The very first command given to man from God recorded in the Bible is found in Genesis 1:28 (ESV): "And God blessed them. And God said to them, 'Be fruitful and multiply and fill the earth and subdue it, and have dominion over the fish of the sea and over the birds of the heavens and over every living thing that moves on the earth.'" The key word in this verse pertaining to a discussion of good government is the word "dominion." From the Hebrew word *rada*, it means to rule. This definition of *rada* is used

> some twenty-two times in the Old Testament, occurring in every section and type of context. The initial usage appears in Gen. 1:28. . . . Generally *rada* is limited to human rather than divine dominion.[8]

The concept of dominion is important when discussing inalienable rights because it reminds us of the importance of man taking charge of his world and subduing it. This is partial support for the right to private property. Taking dominion of the earth means, to some degree, taking ownership of it. The Noahic Covenant is an important Biblical covenant which ensures inalienable rights:

> In the biblical worldview, all humans are expected to be bound by the [Noahic] covenant, which obligates them to recognize God's sovereignty, protect human life, and pursue justice on earth, and also endows them with all the basic human rights. Those who refuse to be bound by accepting the obligations of the [Noahic] covenant are thereby not entitled to those basic human rights because they have proclaimed themselves outlaws.[9]

The most important aspect of the Noahic covenant is its prohibition against murder (Genesis 9:6). This is obviously an affirmation of the right to life. Elazar also contends that there are other commands implicit in the Noahic covenant:

> While there is some disagreement as to precisely which commandments are included, it is generally agreed that idolatry, blasphemy, shedding human blood, sexual sins, theft, and eating parts from a living animal are the six prohibitions, while establishing a legal order is the one positive injunction.[10]

This interpretation would therefore provide protection of the inalienable right to property and liberty, since the prohibition against theft protects one's property and the establishment of a legal order would preserve one's freedom. (It is assumed that this legal order would be just, as God is just.)

The Ten Commandments also serve to protect inalienable rights. First of all, they acknowledge that God has all authority (Exodus 20:3 (ESV) "You shall have no other gods before me"). This is the basis of inalienable rights, because only God gives inalienable rights, and only God can take them away. Second, they acknowledge the right to life (Exodus 20:13 (ESV) "You shall not kill"). Third, they protect the right to property in three ways. The first protection is found in Exodus 20:14 (ESV): "You shall not commit adultery." This implies that a person cannot take another man's wife or another woman's husband, because they already belong to someone else. Co-ownership is an implicit aspect of a marital relationship.

---

[8] Harris, Gleason, and Archer, *Theological Workbook*, 833.

[9] Elazar, *Covenant & Polity*, 87.

[10] Ibid., 112.

The second protection is found in Exodus 20:15 (ESV): "You shall not steal," and the third protection is found in Exodus 20:17 (ESV): "You shall not covet your neighbor's house; you shall not covet your neighbor's wife, or his male servant, or his female servant, or his ox, or his donkey, or anything that is your neighbor's." The protection of life and property are the two most obvious rights protected by the Ten Commandments. However, it is a logical progression that a person's right to liberty is therefore protected because if a person's life is protected and his property is protected (which means that he has the freedom to do what he would like with his property), then he has already achieved a certain degree of freedom.

In addition to these specific protections of inalienable rights, the Bible goes further by exhorting each man to love his neighbor as himself and to treat one another in kindness (Exodus 20:16; Leviticus 19:13, 18, Psalms 15:1-3; Romans 13:10, 15:2, I Corinthians 13). It can safely be argued that no man would want his life, liberty, or property taken away from him, so, according to the Bible, he should not try to take those rights away from others.

Many important political writers have spoken of the need for government to ensure justice. Martin Luther, for instance, in his text, *Church, State, and Citizenship*, states that government must prevent human evil: "If this restraining power were removed—seeing that the entire world is evil and that among thousands there is scarcely one true Christian—men would devour one another, and no one could preserve wife and child, support himself, and serve God. Thus, the world would be reduced to chaos."[11] Likewise, John Calvin, in his *Institutes of the Christian Religion*, argues that government should uphold justice for all, and that it should have the power to defend all citizens from abuse:

> For if power has been given to them [the government] to maintain the tranquillity of their subjects, repress the seditious movements of the turbulent, assist those who are violently oppressed, and animadvert [sic] on crimes, can they rise it more opportunity than in repressing the fury of him who disturbs both the ease of individuals and the common tranquillity of all; who excites seditious tumult, and perpetrates acts of violent oppression and gross wrongs? . . . Natural equity and duty, therefore, demand that princes be armed not only to repress private crimes by judicial inflictions, but to defend the subjects committed to their guardianship whenever they are hostilely assailed. Such even the Holy Spirit, in many passages of Scripture, declares to be lawful.[12]

Sir William Blackstone, one of the most well-known commentators on the British common law, agreed that the "principal aim of society is to protect individuals in the enjoyment of those absolute rights, which were vested in them by the immutable laws of nature, but which could not be preserved in peace without that mutual assistance and intercourse, which is gained by the institution of friendly and social communities."[13]

---

[11] W 11, 251- E22, 68-SL10, 382 in 1 Plass 296 para 867.

[12] Calvin, book Fourth, paragraph/section 11.

[13] Blackstone, Commentaries on the Law of England, Book One, Chapter One, "Of the Absolute Rights of Individuals."

The Multi-Faceted Conundrum of Sin

Despite having these inalienable rights, we are also sinful because we have rejected God's perfect ways. We have spent a good deal of Part I of this book discussing the ways of the orphan, rebel, and slave as manifestations of these sinful tendencies. All of these problems fester even greater manifestations of hate and injustice at the level of government and politics. Sin is not just about actions that we take, but also attitudes of the heart. In fact, the Bible describes sin as an active, confounding force that binds us in spiritual blindness and oppression. Injustice in the world derives from the presence of sin in our lives (Romans 7:17-25). One way this sin nature manifests itself is via a petulant, self-righteous attitude that puts personal rights and freedoms above loving and caring for others. This goes back to the lies of self-sufficiency and a perception that we are better than others. A society in which this attitude is manifest is a dying, decrepit society, where pleasure and ease are pursued at the expense of robust, covenantal engagement with others. This problem then leads to a major conundrum about the sin and the role of the State.

Because of the presence of sin, government is needed. But it also must be limited, because government leaders are also sinful. Rule by consent, separation of powers, checks and balances, use of a Constitution, and federalism are all means to limit the sinfulness of would-be rulers (these ideas will be discussed further below).

Meanwhile, given the spiritual problem of sin, no policy issue should ignore the spiritual component of any problem. Any rejection of the spiritual component of problems, particularly those involving human behavior and matters of the heart, will lead to failed policy interventions. And the conundrum continues: every policy problem has a spiritual dimension, but government cannot address that spiritual dimension; only Christ can. Thus, government, at best, can only restrain evil through the passage and enforcement of laws and regulations. But the more laws and regulations are created, the less freedom and flexibility exists for citizens, and the more likely it is that rulers will seek to consolidate power through new rules, whether by executive, legislative, or judicial fiat.

But wait, there is more: government interventions in society, whether they be economic, domestic, or educational, will have limited success because leaders and citizens alike are irrational due to the power of sin. Even the most logical policy plans will fail because even our capacity for rational thought is limited due to sin and frailty. Economic and domestic solutions which limit government interventions are more apt to be successful simply because they allow for greater involvement of more people with more freedom. Top-down, hierarchical solutions, no matter how good the original intentions of the policy formulators, are apt to fail because political actors, by nature of being sinful and human, will, even with the best of intentions, fail to properly account for all of the complexities of human behavior, social and cultural interactions, and political ramifications of policies.

Even in the best of cases, the law of unintended consequences is a cruel mistress and many policies have fallen prey to it. But in the worst of cases, politicians and law makers tend to use policy initiatives to preserve their own political power. Experts presume to know more than citizens, which is often the case, but not to the point that experts should not be open to dissent, thoughtful dialogue, and the need to augment, tweak, and reform policies. Just as in any organization, so it is with a nation: people who are impacted by a policy should have a say in that policy.

A related evil is that of rent-seeking, where business leaders seek to curry favor with politicians, and vice versa. Government funding and favor, at the expense of the free-market competition leads to cronyism and abuse of power. The free market allows people to use their God-given gifts and talents as they see fit, so long as they are bringing value to the consumer. Too often government rules and regulations favor big business and stymie initiative and creativity. Here again is the problem of putting the State as sovereign above individual liberty and more importantly, above God's law.

Obviously, given that this conundrum is so complex and multifaceted, it can be difficult to divine how best to empower the State to prevent evil while not enabling tyranny. One concept that can help us better understand the proper domain of the State is the **sin-crime distinction**; specifically:

All crimes are sins, but not all sins are crimes.

The State prosecutes and tries to prevent crimes. Crimes are only those sins that comprise a violation of inalienable rights, whether a person's own inalienable rights (suicide, addictive/destructive behaviors, etc.) or the inalienable rights of others.

If we understand that we as individuals may only use physical force to protect ourselves and others in extreme, life-threatening circumstances, we understand that the same is true of the State as well—it can only use its God-given authority and force to prevent crimes which amount to violations of inalienable rights. Meanwhile, the Church, in participation with the power of God's Word and Spirit, seeks to address other types of sin which do not equate to crime. Matters of conscience and personal obedience to the Lord, therefore, cannot be coerced with political or physical power; otherwise, the State will again abuse its power and engage in tyranny.

Historical Developments

As promised, we will now focus on how these important concepts manifested throughout history. This story will tell the tale of how even great empires and political powers bow the knee to God's sovereign plan. It will also reveal the importance of ideas and people who are passionate for the truth. If philosophers and scholars are judged by God, it will be because they entertained foolish, dangerous notions at the expense of God's law. But it will certainly not be because they sought to elicit the truth in nuanced and complex ways, for that is what life requires.

With respect to the development of inalienable rights as a legal framework, we will see that scholars and philosophers played their role well. The development of a theory of inalienable rights took a huge step forward during the Medieval era when jurists and canon lawyers modified Roman law to develop a new theory of property rights according to a Biblical worldview. Medieval jurists and canon lawyers used two Roman legal terms—*dominium* and *ius*—to posit the statement that every person has a right (*ius*) to his property (*dominium*).[14] Initially, in pre-imperial Rome, dominium was used to describe a man's total control over his property. *Ius*, meanwhile, described an inherent standard of rightness or a right ruling. Eventually, however, as Rome shifted into an empire, and as the Emperor gained more power, it should not be surprising to see how these two terms shifted to fit the new political realities. *Ius* came to signify something one possessed as a result of one's political or public standing, particularly via the Emperor. Note the shift—when the State is sovereign, there is no inherent guidance of eternal law; only might makes right. Thus, only one's connections to the rich and powerful guarantee any protection. In turn, *dominium* came to be seen as a type of *ius* via relationships with the Emperor. In other words, in order for an individual to have *dominium* of any sort, he had to have an *ius* as a result of his relationship with the Emperor.

However, after the fall of Rome in 476 AD, the Catholic Church asserted itself as a social, political, and unifying force in Western Europe. We will discuss the negative implications of this in the next section, but here we will note that a Christianized version of the relationship to *dominium* and *ius* laid the foundation for our understanding of inalienable rights. *Ius* came to be seen as something every one possessed as a result of being made in God's image. So eventually, it came to be seen as not specific to being a Christian but being a human. This in turn set the stage for *dominium* to again be linked back to a sense of personal (and therefore private) property ownership. This emphasis in turn lead to an emphasis on caring for the poor (regardless of their lack of political and economic connections with elites).

Upon this concept of man's rights being related to his personhood came the view that man's inalienable rights fall under the categories of life, liberty, and property. Sir William Blackstone wrote that man's rights consist in "the right of personal security, the right of personal liberty; and the right of private property." He considered these rights to be "inviolate." This same understanding was captured by America's Declaration of Independence, which states:

> We hold these truths to be self-evident, that all men are created equal, that they are endowed by their Creator with certain unalienable Rights, that among these are Life, Liberty, and the pursuit of Happiness. That to secure these rights, Governments are instituted among Men, deriving their just powers from the consent of the governed. That whenever any Form of Government becomes destructive of these ends, it is the Right of the People to alter or to abolish it, and to institute new Government, laying its foundation on such principles and organizing its owners in such form, as to them shall seem most likely to effect their Safety and Happiness.

Let us acknowledge that this history of legal terminology was certainly tedious, and even this overview is quite brief and hits only the main ideas of this legal and theological transformation. But it was an important discussion to have to show the link between social, political, and

---

[14] Richard Tuck, *Natural Rights Theories* (New York: Cambridge University Press, 1979), 13.

economic changes made in the Roman Empire, through further changes made in the Medieval era, to finally the formation of a new government in America. The fully developed idea of inalienable rights certainly did not happen overnight. They certainly were not the result of one successful political campaign, and in fact, they did not result from one political leader or party driving the change. In many cases, the shifts and evolution of ideas were the result of indirect circumstances which only a sovereign God could portend. And that is the point: to stay engaged in the political process, pushing for change and reform, while also trusting that in the end, only God is worth trusting.

CHAPTER 7
Corporate Facets of Justice, Society and Government

The Conundrum of Legislation Morality (or Trying Not To)

I need to describe to you what it was like to be a public policy graduate student in the late 90's, as a conservative Christian. The "Pro-Family" movement was at its zenith, with organizations like Focus on the Family, the Family Research Council, the Christian Coalition, and the American Center for Law and Justice wielding considerable political influence and power. The homeschool movement was burgeoning, and the Promise Keepers movement emphasized the importance of men being men—servant leaders walking in integrity and purity, and serving their families (why yes, of course I attended their March in DC). Meanwhile, conservative Christians were entering the political arena—running for and winning elections for local school boards, city councils, state legislators, and Congress. In fact, Congress had already flipped to Republican control, thanks in no small measure to Newt Gingrich's "Contract with America". It was just a matter of time when either Clinton would be impeached (no matter that he and Gingrich were just a few small steps away from rolling out an initiative to privatize Social Security), or barring that, would lose re-election, giving the Party of the pro-life, pro-family movement control of the White House and Congress. And what would be left after all of this? Only the Second Coming.

Those on the Left, of course, were stigmatized and often disgusted by the pro-family movement, and often warned that we should not use government to legislate morality. Even without taking time to discuss how even the best of movements can be co-opted or tokenized by political leaders, there still remains the need to wrestle with that important question legislating morality. On the first day of my government classes in college, I ask my students that very question: whether the State should ever attempt such a thing. There are almost always two general answers. The first is that it would be unfair to force one's morals on others, even unjust to do so. True enough. But the second response follows, just as true, that every law is inherently a moral, even the most archaic tax code, because it assumes that it is good and important to support one's government financially. Even the argument that one should not force morals on others is itself a moral one that has legislative outcomes! So the first question—should we legislate morality?—always leads to a second one: if we cannot help but legislate morality, which morals should be legislated?

What follows is an attempt to answer that question—what morals should the State mandate? Chapter 6 discussed the implications for the State predicated upon what we can derive from our relationship with God. This is in keeping with the book's theme that we must always start with our identity—who are as made in God's image, and how that identity must be acknowledged and protected by the State. Though this sense of *imago dei* clearly has deeply personal and spiritual implications, it just as clearly has implications for the role of the State, as discussed in chapter 6. This chapter continues that discussion and moves into the impacts of how we engage with one another and care for one another, or at least how we should. And yes, that will inevitably involve "legislating morality"—it cannot be helped. But it will be argued here that because of the institutional separation of Church and State, discussed below, minimizes impositions onto personal freedom.[1]

The Relationship between God and Man: Covenant and Church-State Relations

This section surely generates some controversy. In the preface of the book, I offered a brief greeting to those on the Left—people who have had enough of cultural, statist exploitation of minorities, often fueled by religious oppression, particularly a culture, ostensibly supported and affirmed by "the Church," which is predicated upon evils such as chauvinism, racism, and elitism. I of course put the "the Church" in quotes because there is nothing Churchly and nothing Christian, about any of those evils. And while we need not swallow whole cloth sweeping judgments and decrees that Christianity and life in the Church is inherently chauvinistic or racist, I do believe it can be easy for a Church to support those types of evils if it abandons the grace of God for a legalistic, perfectionistic, self-sufficiency.

This problem is akin to the problem of the Pharisees—the white-washed tombs of their day, as Christ called them (Matthew 23:27-28). He had little regard for their sense of righteousness. They had become infatuated with the approval of men and their own social status. Their pedantic attention to the Law often came at the expense of the spirit of the Law which of course is to love God with all that we are and to love one another as we love ourselves (Matthew 22:37-40). Instead, they exchanged that for a works-based, prideful approach which did indeed lead to devaluing women, particularly through favoring a hair-trigger approach to divorce and disowning women, disregarding the poor and even one's parents. If this type of "faith" was a problem in Christ's time, and if he devoted significant attention to it, we should probably as well, in our time.

---

[1] I bet you thought I was going to mention falling sleep in class again, as if a joke becomes more humorous the more you tell it, like beating a dead horse is funnier. But I'm not going to do so, because I have no desire *whatsoever* to give my classmate and erstwhile canoe rental business partner, Bob Wallace, any credit for his tomfoolery. You see, when I would inevitably fall asleep in class in grad school, on the front row no less, he would surreptitiously pour a bit of water right in front of me, so that when I woke up (which I did, because I cared and was a diligent student!), I would think I had drooled and then I would try to nonchalantly wipe it up. It took me *months* to figure out what was going on, and all the while my so-called friend would giggle like a little school child. Not funny, Bob, not funny at all.

One way of doing so is drawing attention to how this religion of legalistic, perfectionistic, self-sufficiency manifests itself in the political arena via an *institutional* fusion of Church and State. This text may not agree with those on the Left with respect to full nature of the problem of exploitation in a couple of ways. First, the true cause of the problem is not structural—it is not first and foremost about moneyed, powerful interests exploiting everyone else, though we would be foolish to ignore that this is a very real and abiding problem. It is just that the issue first and foremost is spiritual. And since it is a spiritual problem, common to all humans, we do well to avoid the radical rage which seeks only to judge and not to make peace with God, either on a personal level or on a greater level. The world does not need more angry, self-righteous judges who proclaim to be able to properly judge all.

Second, the solutions proposed by the Left also undermine the very limitations put upon government which would further limit tyranny and freedom. Removing private property, for instance, stifles human agency, creativity, and liberty. Removing a judicial process which focuses on actions, not intents, and killing and people who are seen as allies to the prevailing economic system would also be tyrannical and unjust. Removing freedom of speech in the name of preventing exploitation becomes its own exploitation, its own evil. However, having said all of that, there should be at least one common point of agreement here: *the institutional fusion of Church and State is one of the greatest sources of oppression mankind has known.* Minimally, it contributes to a culture where so-called religious leaders adorn themselves in the trappings of social and political status at the expense of others. This type of church seeks the favor of those in power, while at the same time seeking to use the political, coercive power of the State to compel others to obey their rules and regulations.

This is not the Church of Jesus Christ, the Servant God who humbled himself so that we might be saved. He presents himself as gentle and merciful and offers us his own yoke-bearing strength so that as we obey him, we might be freed and empowered by him (Matthew 11:28-30). Following and accepting the Gospel of Jesus Christ, then, cannot be coerced. It is far too precious, far too intimate, to be arbitrarily conceived by political fiat. It is true that secularists and Postmodernists fear any influence of Christianity in government functions and thus often seek to remove any vestige of Christian thought from the public square. This, as has been argued throughout this text, has dire consequences for any society.

But it is also true that to the extent that they are concerned about the type of religion described above, they are right to be concerned and we should be concerned right along with them. As more than aside, it was this ethos that allowed Christians in the American South to link their own view of religion into an idolized culture, where family, the land, and tradition justified a paternalistic slavery. This institutional fusion of Church and State is the legalism, pride and self-sufficiency come to full fruition. We must fight it and uproot it from our hearts and our society, in all of its political, social, manifestations. Following, then, is a brief description of how it operates and some historical trends in the development of institutional separation of these two sacred realms.

The fusion of Church and State can come in two general forms. One mode is the *Church over the State*, as was seen in Medieval Europe with the papacy often controlling the Holy Roman Empire and the like, as well what is seen in some modern Muslim nations today.

The *State over the Church* can be seen in tyrannies such as the former Soviet Union, China, and indeed any nation that thwarts freedom of conscience and religious expression as we often see today, even in America. To the extent that secularists have gained legal provisions to deny freedom of conscience in modern America and elsewhere is the extent to which the State is ruling over the Church today. In either case, the coercive power of the State is used to force people against their freedom of conscience, their freedom of religion, and their liberty. Imagine if Christ came to earth and used military power and might to force people to obey Him. He did not do this, and in fact did not use his own divine power to do so. Instead, he died for our sins. In keeping with God's covenantal approach to humans, made in his image, we are all called to freely choose to serve God through Christ. There can be no coercion in coming to God, as we know. The saving work of Christ must be freely accepted.

Thus, the State must not infringe upon matters of conscience, nor must the Church have the ability to coerce people via the power of the State into obeying Scripture. Additionally, and no small matter, is that in the past, competition between the Church and State has often led to war and bloodshed. Although we do not necessarily deal with that same type of conflict in society today, we do struggle with the dilemma of the proper relationship between these two realms of authority. Is it appropriate to espouse Biblical principles in government? What influence should the State have upon the Church and vice versa? These are just a few of the questions that Christians and non-Christians alike must answer to ensure that both institutions are able to fulfill their proper roles in society. One of the ways we have tried to answer some of these questions is noting that the sin-crime distinction properly limits both the Church and the State from over-stepping their bounds. Further, the following discussion will reveal that the Church and State should be separate institutions, and that they should respect one another's sovereignty and try not to interfere with one another's God-given responsibilities.

The Church and State Must Have Separate Functions

First, we know that both the Church and State have divinely assigned duties. The New Testament commentary on the role of government can first be found in the Gospels (Matthew 22:15-22, Mark 12:13-17, Luke 20:20-26), where Jesus Christ addresses the question of the validity of paying taxes to Caesar. His answer, of course, is to "render therefore unto Caesar the things which are Caesar's [i.e., pay your taxes]; and unto God the things that are God's [i.e., pay your tithes and offerings]" (Matthew 22:21, Mark 12:17, Luke 20:25). What we see in Christ's comments, then, is both an affirmation of the State, but also a limitation upon the State, since not everything belongs to it. In fact, while the coin Christ referenced bore the image of Caesar, we humans bear the image of God, and thus to God alone we belong, and not the State.

The Church, meanwhile, is called to make disciples of all men and to point mankind to Christ. The State, on the other hand, has been given the sword of judgement. Romans 13:1-4 describes government officials as being ministers. Another key passage is 1 Peter 2:13-17 (ESV), which states that Christians should:

> Be subject for the Lord's sake to every human institution, whether it be to the emperor as supreme, or to governors as sent by him to punish those who do evil and to praise those who do good. For this is the will of God, that by doing good you should put to silence the ignorance of foolish people. Live as people who are free, not using your freedom as a cover-up for evil, but living as servants of God. Honor everyone. Love the brotherhood. Fear God. Honor the emperor.

In turn, since we are going to talk about swords, we could say that the Church bears the (symbolic) "sword" of excommunication, meaning it is called to lovingly discipline and correct fellow Christians who risk disobeying God and abandoning the faith, in keeping with passages such as Matthew 18:15-17. The Church is to convict the world of its sin, and draw all men unto repentance through Jesus Christ. Only the Church, which is made up of the children of God, can do this. Likewise, only the State can punish someone for crime.

The difference between the roles of the Church and State, therefore, arise from the difference between *sin* and *crime*, as mentioned earlier. All crimes are sins, but not all sins are crimes. Crimes represent a violation of the life, liberty, and property (inalienable rights), of others. We infer that the violations of these rights equate to an existential threat to our existence, and thus is the only time we can use force against others. When Christ told his followers to turn the other cheek (Matthew 5:38-40), note a clear difference between a slap in the face and a loss of life. We will discuss the Biblical notion of self-defense below—again these principles do overlap and it can be difficult to know which one to present first.

This parameter also generally limits the State's use of force. If it oversteps this role, it will find itself acting like the Church, and trying to coerce people against their freedom of conscience and liberty. Based on our discussion of covenantal relationships, we know that every person, group, and institution have certain responsibilities given to them by God which only they can perform. The relationship between Church and State is no exception to this rule. The Church should only involve itself in its God-given responsibilities, and nothing else, as should the State. This institutional separation is even found in, of all places, the Old Testament Mosaic law, which clearly stated that priests could never become kings, and kings could never perform priestly functions (2 Chronicles 26:19). There is a clear division of authority. Meanwhile, prophets also would be called upon by God to speak against corrupt kings (and the people) whenever they violated God's laws.

This leads to our next point—the Church should never be the patron of the State. It should never seek financial or coercive support from the State. The moment it does is the moment it becomes a tool of the State. From the dawn of time, rulers have used religion as a cloak with which to wrap themselves as they sought the fear and adoration of the people. Tyrants love churches—so long as the churches love them—so that in turn the churches can be used to further the agenda of those tyrants. For those concerned about ideas such as "Christian nationalism," here is your fear realized: when a tyrants use religious imagery, supported by the nation's churches, to justify their tyrannical, imperial, and coercive actions.

Separation of Church and State Does Not Mean a Separation of the State from Biblical Principles

Arguing for an institutional separation of Church and State does not mean that we should not seek to enforce a Biblical perspective of government, of course. Without the eternal, transcendent truths of God's Word, we would essentially only have rule by might in some form or fashion, or we would have anarchy. It is popular to argue that "you can't legislate morality." This assumes that there is somehow an ability to write and pass a law which does not have some appeal to morality, whether good or bad. That is simply not possible. For instance, even the most arcane tax code assumes a moral that it is good to give of one's earnings to the State.

There is always a value assessment made with each and every law. It is only from a Biblical framework that we see that the only morals which should be legalized—that is, should be enforced by coercive power of the State, and not the reforming power of the Church—relate to the protection of inalienable rights and the basic administration of justice. So, in short, a Biblical perspective on the relations between the Church and State actually maximizes individual freedom and gives people the most space to live their lives as they see fit, so long as they do not bring harm to their neighbor. In today's pluralistic society, where Christianity is far from the supreme cultural influence, it is no small irony that a Biblical worldview provides the most accommodations for such plurality, even as many decry that same worldview.

Historical Evidence

The fusion of Church and State, in one way or another, has been the historical norm. Remember again the comment about ancient history and how emperors sought to use religion. Often these rulers portrayed themselves as gods to be worshiped. Christ upturned all of this when he introduced a kingdom fueled not by the cut of the swords of soldiers, but by the piercing, dividing work of the Holy Spirit in our very heart of hearts, to draw us to repentance (Hebrews 4:12). Again, the Lord always works from the inside out. As the early Church grew and spread throughout the Roman Empire, persecution arose, but it was ended by Emperor Constantine, who himself converted to Christianity. We can debate whether or not his conversion was sincere, but that is the goal of someone else's book. In any case, it becomes increasingly clear that the Roman Empire saw Christianity as a tool to be wielded. Whereas Constantine ended persecution and made Christianity legal (a designation which may have pulled the church out of authentic, Christ-abiding faith into more of a cultural, political, and social engagement), Emperor Theodosius made it the only official religion. Thus, the institution fusion of the Christian Church with the State of the Roman Empire began. It is true that Justinian, at least to some extent, used Biblical principles to reform and reorganize Roman legal code. This is commendable, but did not remove the problem of the institutional fusion.

However, when Rome fell in AD 476, it began a trend, at least in Western Europe, of breaking part this institutional fusion. First, the Roman Catholic Church split from the Greek Orthodox Church in AD 1054. Part of the reason for the split was that the Roman Catholic

Church took issue with the influence of the Eastern Byzantine emperor in church affairs.[2] Of course, we also know that the Roman Catholic Church simultaneously desired its own political power and control, and sought to subvert the will of kings and princes to its own. This was still a fusion of Church and State, but at least we begin to see an initial point of separation. In fact, in 1122 AD, the Investiture Controversy led to a further separation of Church and State as the king and pope argued over who had the right to invest religious leaders with authority. There was fighting, yes, but also further institutional separation in the wake of the resolution of this debate.[3]

Centuries later, the Protestant Reformers, having seen the corruption of the Catholic Church, and particularly how it used the influence of kings and princes to attempt to coerce Protestants to renounce their convictions, further articulated a doctrine of institutional separation. For too long, Catholic kings and popes alike had resisted the freedom of religion advocated for by various Christians, starting with the Morning Star of the Reformation, John Wycliffe himself. The Protestant Reformation led to many political leaders seeking to break away from the control of the Catholic Church. There were many confrontations and much bloodshed, most notably the Thirty Years War. Many Protestants from all over Europe were persecuted for their faith; that is, the political, coercive power of the State was brought to bear in an attempt to cause them to recant. Many of these Protestants fled to the New World. As America began to assert their own independence, they had plenty of reasons, therefore, to call for a true institutional separation of Church and State: there would be no more state-sponsored churches in America. It also helped, incidentally, that the first Great Awakening, which happened spontaneously and without any directive of a state Church, simultaneously increased religious fervor while weakening state-sponsored churches.[4] After all, if you serve the living God, you do not need the State to prop up your faith or your religious institutions. And as scholar John Eidsmoe points out, the Founding Fathers

> professed and exhibited a deep faith in God. They believed not only in a God of creation, but also in a God who is active in human history. . . . At least eight and probably eleven believed Jesus Christ is the Son of God. . . . The founding fathers were students of the Bible. They quoted it authoritatively and made frequent allusions to Scripture in their writings and speeches. . . . All of the founding fathers except Jefferson concurred with the Bible that man is basically sinful and self-centered; they did recognize that man is capable of certain civic virtue (Ro. 2:14-15). . . . All thirteen of the founding fathers had great respect for organized religion, particularly Christianity. . . . The founding fathers who did not choose to be Christians expressed gratitude for Christianity's influence within their nation. If the founding fathers

---

[2] Yvves Congar, *After Nine Hundred Years* (New York: Fordham University Press, 1959), 11.

[3] Harold Berman, *The Origin of the Western Legal Tradition* (Cambridge, England: Harvard University Press, 1983), 98.

[4] Angela Kamrath, *The Miracle of America: The Influence of the Bible on the Founding History and Principles of the United States of America for a People of Every Belief,* Second Edition (Houston, TX: American Heritage Education Foundation, 2014).

were to see the hostile contempt with which modern thinkers treat Christianity, I believe they would consider it strange, offensive, and self-destructive.[5]

Of course, any mention of the Founders requires a mention of slavery, and how they handled that. We will discuss this in a future section. But for now, we will pivot to a discussion of how covenantal principles, of which the institutional separation of Church and State is one, should further be manifest in society. We are discussing this now because we are moving away from a discussion of how God manifests his work in society (i.e., a rejection of state power to coerce faith and obedience) to how we should live in covenant with one another.

Man and Man: Covenant, Mutual Accountability, Federalism, and Noncentralization

Review

The notion of covenant is again a great starting point to transition between the implications of government based upon our relationship with God (chapter 6) and in turn, our relationship with one another (chapter 7). We have already discussed the key facets of covenantal theology in Chapters 2 and 6. To continue the conversation, there are four key concepts from the covenantal paradigm—indeed inherent to it—which are quite applicable to a discussion of government, politics, and statecraft. The first is the idea of **hesed**—loving fulfillment of covenant obligation. *Hesed* is the ethos behind the covenantal ideal. It provides a foundation for laws and regulations by affirming the importance not just of the letter of the law, but also the spirit of the law, and in so doing, it saves us from the practice of looking for grey areas and legal loopholes while also avoiding the tendency to over-regulate and over-stipulate. Because in fact, the tendency to look for ethical grey areas and hiding spots in the law fuels the tendency to create lengthy, confusing, obscure contractual terminology and legalize and to create regulations upon regulations in attempt to prevent bad behavior.

We are here reminded that only Christ can reform the heart of human. Find a society whose members are far away from the Lord, and you will find a society with either anarchy or excessive laws and regulations. Or both. But a people who know the person of *Hesed*, that is Christ, understand that true righteousness is owned to God in "spirit and in truth" (John 4:23-24) which further obligates them to love their neighbor by turning the other cheek, going the extra mile, and loving their neighbors as themselves. The children of God understand these important ideas because they understand that Christ personified *hesed* on the cross. He modeled for us how to love God and love others. So we can see that the biblical-covenantal idea of *hesed* goes hand-in-hand with pairing of liberty and self-government. Self-governing people are not controlled by the tyranny of sin and thus does not seek to tyrannize others, and nor would they seek to shirk their duties to others or hide behind some sort of contractual

---

[5] John Eidsmoe, Christianity and the Constitution: The Faith of Our Founding Fathers (Grand Rapids, MI: Baker Books, 1987), 341–2.

terminology to avoid doing so. For a child of God, one's covenantal obligations is not just a duty, it is an act of love. Thus, the bondage of selfish individualism—and it is bondage because it is sin—is also rejected.

This informs the second key concept, which is **mutual accountability**. We are accountable to one another as neighbors and as citizens. We are accountable to the laws of the land, so long as they are righteous, and not just the letter of the law, but the spirit. Our leaders and elected officials are accountable to us as well, which is why so often wherever we see covenantal attributes at work in a society, you also see some form of representative government, and wherever we find the absence of covenantal principles in a society, we see a hindrance of democracy, even when it is allegedly present. For instance, a democracy which undermines the rights of people, or which affirms some travesty like slavery, undermines liberty and self-government.

With any sound democracy you have the third covenantal concept, which is **constitutionalism**. A covenantal relationship is built upon non-coercive, mutually affirming relationships. This ensures that everyone's rights are protected, and that processes and structures empower rather than oppress people. Just as the book of Deuteronomy was essentially the constitution of the Mosaic Code and the people of Israel, so do modern constitutions seek to affirm the covenantal basis of the rights of the people and the limitations of leaders and government agencies. This constitution should also be based on God's immutable law, specifically the affirmation of the *imago dei* of each person and inalienable rights. In this way, a constitution not only protects us from the tyranny of leaders, but also the tyranny of the mobs. Majority rule should never supersede inalienable rights.

Finally, covenantal systems of government are also **non-centralized**. A key aspect of federalism, this idea, as noted earlier, is not the same as decentralization, which merely speaks to how "flat" an organizational system is. Rather, non-centralization speaks to a system, a society, where power comes from the people to the government and where power within the government is separated and shared, and finally, where various centers of power exist throughout the system. These "spheres" of sovereignty do not exist as extensions of the State, nor are they entirely beholden to the State. And the State itself is just one of many spheres, which includes individual citizens, families, churches, localities, non-profits, and other types of governments, such as the individual states, in the American context, each of which has its own sphere of sovereignty or autonomy over which the other spheres may not trample. All of these spheres interact with one another, sharing power, cooperating with one another, upholding justice, and securing the common good.

This diversified, covenantal empowerment is both messy and effective at both limiting tyranny and ensuring national resiliency. But for the ideal to work, it assumes that all of the spheres are in fact actively seeking to cooperate with one another to achieve liberty and justice for all. This has not always been the case. The southern states resisted the Civil Rights movement where inalienable rights were very much being thwarted, for example. Thus, noncentralization can be used to hinder progress and liberty. But removing noncentralization and giving too much power a central government will absolutely do the same and more. True, noncentralization is less than efficient, but government by the people and for the people was never meant to be efficient; it was meant to be effective at securing liberty and justice for all. It requires robust self-government, which in turn requires active and constant engagement, participation, and collaboration.

It requires a lot, and for many people, the notion of freedom is the notion to be left alone. In contrast, the biblical idea of liberty is not being left alone, but rather using one's liberty to serve one another (1 Peter 2:15-17). So this active, engaged, messy, complicated process and structure of noncentralization is not linear, nor does it always lead to consensus. But what exasperates tyrants, elites, and bureaucrats empowers the people, so long as the people are willing to use that empowerment to love their neighbors (all of them), care for and strengthen their communities, and prevent exploitation. With these concepts in mind, let us look at the history of the covenantal idea, both throughout Scripture and as it emerged in the West.

A Progression of Covenants: Creation and Redemption

The covenants of the Old and New Testament can be divided into two "mandates": creation and redemption, both of which coexist and unfold throughout Scripture simultaneously. The Creation Mandate describes the realities of living in a broken, sinful world, where evil and injustice exist and where the State must exist to hopefully thwart and limit such evil (Romans 13:1-7; 1 Timothy 2:1-2; 1 Peter 2:13-17). But simultaneously, Christ has solved the problem of sin and promised that his Church would grow and prosper, even against the gates of Hell (Matthew 16:18). This second reality is known as the Redemption Mandate. One mandate does not obviate the other.

For further explanation, we begin with the Creation mandate, which came into existence in the garden with Adam and Eve and continued with their sin and disobedience against God (Genesis 3). This is where sin first occurred (, and yes, where the plan of redemption through Christ was offered (Genesis 3:14-15; Romans 5:12-21). The problem of sin reminds us that despite the advent of the New Kingdom, and the *Redemption* that comes with it, we are still in need of the State. Sin entered the world through Adam (at the onset of *Creation*), and ever since, we have needed government to prevent rampant crime and exploitation. That would imply that facets of the State, such as police forces and the military, are also still needed. And yet, because of sin, all of these can and have been misused. We should neither ignore that in a misguided call for patriotism and loyalty, nor should we pretend that they should be abolished.

Meanwhile, the plan of redemption was echoed in the Noahic covenant (Genesis 9:12-16), and then in the Abrahamic (Genesis 15), Mosaic (the laws, ceremonies, and sacrificial system of the people of Israel, ultimately fulfilled in Christ), and Davidic covenants (2 Samuel 7:8-16; Mark 10:47). Finally, the New Covenant ushered in the final and complete work of Christ. As we further understand the progression of covenants from the Old to New Testament in Scripture, we see that the New Testament does not espouse a theocracy as Israel had in the Old Testament, in the Mosaic covenant. The New Covenant of Jesus Christ affirms and supersedes the previous covenants of the Old Testament. The New Covenant affirms the old covenants by recognizing God's intent in each covenant. It supersedes those past covenants by bringing God's plan for redemption to completion in the death and resurrection of Christ. The Holy Spirit is now at work drawing people to repentance through the work of the Church . This being the case, there are still two obstacles to avoid.

The first is to obviate all prior covenants. If these have all been totally replaced by the New Covenant, then perhaps there would be no need for government at all, since Christ has come and his kingdom is now here. And yet, sin came through Adam, and it still exists in the world today, as we have already discussed. Further, Christ himself (Matthew 22:21), along with New Testament passages affirm the divinely assigned role of the State. So we reject antinomianism outright (Romans 13:1-7; 1 Timothy 2:1-2; 1 Peter 2:13-17). Thus, the Creation mandate is still in effect, even though now we, as sons and daughters of God, are also walking and living within the Redemption mandate. We should also note that the Mosaic covenant naturally proceeds from the Abrahamic covenant, as the people of Israel are indeed Abraham's descendants. But even more so, as Christians, we have been grafted into the tree of Abraham through the work of Christ (Romans 11). Further, in Galatians, Paul explains that the Abrahamic Covenant was one based upon faith first and supersedes the Mosaic law, which existed to explain the depth of our sin and to guard us until the coming of Christ (Galatians 3:19-29). And all of this is in keeping with the premise that one biblical covenant affirms the principles and ideas of the previous covenant; God's character does not change, after all (Numbers 23:19, Matthew 24:35).

This in turn leads us to the second obstacle: if God's character does not change and His laws are eternal, then why are we not still abiding by the laws of Moses? This is a common concern raised by skeptics when they hear Christians talk about government being based on biblical principles. It understandably sends a chill down their spine to think of all the rituals and ceremonies of the Mosaic covenant, to say nothing of the capital punishments meted out to the likes of witches, homosexuals, and even rebellious children. The crucial component for resolving this apparent dilemma is recognizing that the Adamic and Noahic covenants impacted all of humankind and are still relevant (the Creation Mandate), but the Abrahamic, Mosaic, and Davidic covenants are only for the children of God and have ultimately been fulfilled in the New Covenant (the Redemption Mandate). This is true in several ways.

First, all of the *ceremonial* components of Mosaic law related to the temple and sacrifice have of course been fulfilled and obviated by the work of Christ, who is both our faithful High Priest and our sacrificial lamb. The entire book of Hebrews in the New Testament explains this. Likewise, the *judicial* components of the Mosaic code—all of the punishments for various sins as defined by Scripture, have also been fulfilled in Christ's sacrifice on the cross. He bore our sins so that we would not be punished, which is related to the fact that his sacrifice also obviated the need for continual temple sacrifices—the Gospel is good news indeed (Romans 3:21-31)!

Meanwhile, the final component of the Mosaic law—the *moral* code telling us what is right and wrong, specifically as seen in the Ten Commandments, are still in effect, as God's character and righteousness are unfailing and immutable. As prophesied by Jeremiah (31:33-34), this law would eventually be written in our hearts—this inherent sense of right and wrong and the ability to live in accordance with it, would be empowered through the work of the Holy Spirit in our lives. This in turn contributes to our notion of self-government discussed earlier, but more importantly explains how we can resolve any tensions related to the interplay of the Abrahamic, Mosaic, and Davidic covenants into the New Covenant. It probably goes without saying that the Davidic covenant of course was finally and truly fulfilled in Christ who is King David's descendent. Therefore, as mentioned before, it is still appropriate to instill biblical principles in government just as it is in all realms of life. But this assumes a limited scope of government centered on the protection of inalienable rights as well as a covenantal approach rather than the more extensive Mosaic code. In the next section, in turn, we will look at some historical evidence related to these concepts.

Historical Roots of the Covenant Idea

The idea of covenant is almost exclusively a biblical, particularly with respect to the notion of mutual accountability and *hesed*. In the Old Testament, it not only empowered the people of Israel, but gave them the opportunity—and responsibility to choose. In Medieval times, Jewish communities certainly kept alive covenantal traditions[6], even as Catholic Europe overlooked much of the nuance of covenant found in Scripture. This lack of emphasis was possibly due to the Hebrew words for covenant—*brit, berith*, etc.—being translated into the Greek term *diatheke*, which does not capture or convey covenantal ideas such as mutual accountability and *hesed*.[7] From there, *diatheke* was translated into the Latin word *testamentum*, which explains why we refer to the two major sections of the Bible as the Old and New Testaments. A testament, as we know, is more of a one-sided statement of who receives what from the designator. It also fails to emphasize mutual accountability or *hesed*. However, when Jerome translated Scripture directly from the Hebrew to Latin for a new translation of Scripture, he was advised by rabbi scholars who spoke Hebrew Greek and Latin to use more appropriate terms such as *foedus* and *pactum*.[8]

This emphasis on *foedus* in particular was instrumental during the Protestant Reformation for creating a theological, conceptual framework for covenantal or federal theology. This theological approach provided the grounding to talk about institutional separation of Church and State, along with greater freedom of conscience and a rejection of both the concept of divine right of kings as well as the Medieval "chain of being" which asserted a permanent hierarchical structure to society with elites (such as popes and kings) at the top and the commoners at the bottom. A more covenantal approach rejected the political, social, and economic implications of this hierarchy while also, of course, emphasizing the "priesthood of all believers."[9] The political and cultural implications of such an approach explain even more why Protestants in various

---

[6] Daniel J. Elazar, Covenant as the Basis of the Jewish Political Tradition, *The Jewish Journal of Sociology*, 20, no. 1 (1978).

[7] Gordon. M. Freeman, "The Dark Side of Covenant," Workshop on Covenant and Politics, Temple University (December 1980).

[8] James B. Torrance, "The Covenant Concept in Scottish Theology and Politics," Workshop on Covenant and Politics, Temple University (February 1980).

[9] Michael Walzer, *The Revolution of the Saints: A Study in the Origins of Radical Politics* (Cambridge: Harvard University Press, 1965), 168–169.

nations of Europe were persecuted for their faith. Many of these Protestants came to the New World and they brought there covenantal thinking with them. Over time, the church covenants or compacts that established new colonies also established political guidelines and structures, including the constitutions of the various states. These constitutions and covenantal ideas eventually became the basis of America's federal or covenantal structure. They transcended church life and influenced the rise of modern organizations in America. Elazar wrote that

> Scientific and reform societies, labor unions, and professional associations as well as business corporations were formed on the basis of compacts or contracts. In many cases, they also contracted with one another to form larger organizations while preserving their own integrities. In so doing, they extended federalization into new nongovernmental areas, a pattern which continues to this day.[10]

The covenant idea, introduced in the Bible, rediscovered in the Middle Ages, articulated in the Reformational Era, and reinforced in the American founding and Westward expansion continues today throughout the world:

> Today some forty percent of the world's population lives within the 19 polities which have adopted constitutions that at least purport to be federal in character, while another 32 percent live within the 18 political systems which utilize federal principles to some degree within a formally unitary framework. If we were to add into our calculations supranational federal arrangements, such as the European Community, the number of polities would be even larger and the share of the world's population directly touched by the federalist revolution substantially increased. While the variety of forms which the federalist revolution has taken is great, the American federal system remains the single most influential standard against which all others are measured, for better or worse.[11]

It is no surprise then that a covenantal perspective on life and society also lead to a theory of civil resistance against tyranny. This is the last topic of this chapter.

Selfless Self-Defense: Resisting Tyranny

Overview

Adam and Eve, being made in God's image, were called to be fruitful and to multiply and to take dominion (Genesis 1:26-31). This implies the use of property and liberty to do so. But it was to be done in obedience to God and out of worship, not for selfish ends. Self-defense then should occur as a means of restraining evil. If we allow someone to kill us, for instance, when we had the ability to stop them, we would be undermining our ability to serve God. And if

---

[10] Daniel J. Elazar, "The Political Theory of Covenant: Biblical Origins and Modern Developments," *Publius* 10, no. 4 (1980): 23–24.

[11] Daniel J. Elazar, "The Almost-Covenanted Polity," *Workshop on Covenant and Politics*, 1982, 1.

we do not stop them, they might hurt others as well. So, what we are really talking about is "selfless self-defense"—living our lives for God's glory and living to serve others. In doing so, it could be that we might end up being a martyr, because we will not bow down to evil. But there may be times when actual fighting and military advancement is necessary to stop evil.

Another key point is that self-defense is inimical to a spirit of vengeance and wrath (Romans 12:19). We do not engage in self-defense out of hatred or a spirit of vengeance; rather, we understand that stopping evil is an important way of loving our neighbor, so that they are not exploited. It would also mean setting up a system of justice to stop criminals from hurting the weak and vulnerable in society. Therefore, if we are allowed to use self-defense to protect our lives and our freedoms, it can be argued then that government should also have that power, but that it should be limited primarily to the same realm of authority that we have in defending ourselves or those from serious harm. And that in turn is why protecting inalienable rights is so important—it defines the key things for which we might use self-defense—basic life, liberty, and property.

Government exists first and foremost to protect our inalienable rights and ensure justice. Citizens are required to participate in the political process as a means of limiting tyranny. Because these rights cannot be taken away, government must be limited so it does not overstep its bounds with regards to personal rights. On the other hand, government must be active in protecting these rights. Further, the Bible is clear that we are to love our neighbors as ourselves. We do not violate the inalienable rights of our neighbors because they are made in God's image. But the converse is also true—we are not permitted to violate and purposefully destroy our own inalienable rights, and government in turn is obligated to prevent such self-violations.

This is different from serving as a martyr for God's word or dying on the battlefield. These types of actions are done in service to others and to God. On the contrary, abdicating to evil, whether through some destructive personal behavior such as drug addictions or by allowing tyranny to gain power in a free society, could both be seen as violating one's inalienable rights. An off-shoot of these premises is that humans are called to self-government. We must live in the liberty that comes with obedience to God, lest we become slaves to sin (Romans 6:17-18). Slavery to sin has more than just personal impacts—it either leads us to control and exploit the rights of others or to allow ourselves to be controlled and exploited by tyrants or other oppressors.

What then are citizens supposed to do when their inalienable rights are violated by the state? An understanding of covenantal principles offers guidelines for such a scenario. We know that in a covenantal relationship, all parties involved enter into the agreement by free choice, not by force, and that the rights of all the parties are protected, because the parties have the chance to stipulate that their rights be protected during the negotiation process. We also know that once the covenantal relationship is established, the parties involved must willingly submit to one another in order to fulfill the various requirements of the covenant. Furthermore, we know that the parties to a covenant are not at liberty to break the covenant every time one of the other parties falls short in fulfilling the covenantal obligations. The concept of *hesed*, which is covenantal mercy, denotes an act of forgiveness that should be exhibited among all of the parties. But this act of covenantal mercy has its limits. When one of the parties fails to fulfill his covenantal obligations in a serious matter, thereby negating the very principles upon which the covenant was based, it is then appropriate for the other members to free themselves from their covenant obligations to the violator, and where applicable, to punish or disqualify the violating party from the covenantal agreement and the blessings of the covenant:

> A covenant includes mercy [this mercy is related to *hesed*, in that the members are willing to go the extra mile to preserve the covenant] so that if a party fails to keep the covenant perfectly, it is still valid. However, a particular kind of failure–a material breach of the terms or conditions–frees the injured party from any further obligations under the agreement.[12]

A material breach is akin to someone using force against another to the point of threatening their very life. It is an existential threat. First of all, the Bible discusses many instances where a covenant is annulled due to a material breach of the people: "Adam's eating the forbidden fruit was a material breach of God's covenant of works (Ge. 2:17). Idolatry was a material breach of God's covenant of law on Mount Sinai (Ex. 32). Adultery is a material breach of the covenant of marriage (Mt. 19:9)."[13]

When Christ told us to turn the other cheek (Matthew 5:38-42), he was not referring to this type of threat. Moreover, just as he came to fulfill every aspect of the Law (Matthew 5:18), he by default also affirmed some measure of self-defense that was first established in the Old Testament (Exodus 22: 2-3) even as he clearly rejected a political, military kingdom for himself on the other (Matthew 26:52). And none of this emphasis on self-defense is contrary to a heart attitude that calls out for mercy for one's enemies. Self-defense is not hatred, nor should it be fueled by a spirit of vengeance.

These principles can be applied to a situation where the covenant is between the state and the people, and the state begins to overreach its covenantally-proscribed powers by violating the inalienable rights of the people, or by trying to lead the people into disobedience of God's law. We know that all government should be based on an acknowledgment of and obedience to God and His Word, the Bible. We also know, therefore, that the purpose of government is to protect the inalienable rights of its citizens and to uphold justice. Therefore, no covenant should violate these principles, even if the covenant involves an entire nation and its government. In the situation described above, the offenses committed by the ruler or state are so egregious to the nature of the covenant and to what is acceptable according to biblical standards that the people are obligated to remedy the situation, even if it means annulling the covenant altogether. However, *hesed* [covenant mercy] can play a role even in this situation.

Also, the Bible provides examples where the covenant of government has been annulled by the leader's evil deeds. One example is found in I Kings 12:1-25, where the people ask King Rehoboam to lighten the taxes. When he disregards their request, and instead promises

---

[12] Gary Amos, *Defending the Declaration* (Charlottesville, VA: Providence Foundation, 1994), 129.

[13] Amos, *Defending*, 129–130.

to be even more severe than his father Solomon was, all of the tribes except Benjamin and Judah rejected the leadership of Rehoboam and formed a new government under Jeroboam, which the Lord approved (vv. 15, 24).

The people, rather than throwing off all civil rule, must turn to those pre-established leaders (who are not violating the covenant) to remedy the situation. In this way the covenant can be preserved with only minor changes. This process is known as interposition and was first articulated by John Calvin.[14] Of course, in the extreme case, where all of the established authority figures are committing material breaches of the covenant, it would be appropriate for the people to totally annul the covenant, to create a new covenant (and therefore establish new leaders), and, if necessary, to fight against the tyranny of the old authorities.

Having said all of this, here are some concluding thoughts on the notion of self-defense. Yes, we should quick to fight against tyranny. Doing so relates back to loving one's neighbor. But part of doing requires acknowledging that tyranny begins in the human heart—we all desire to set ourselves up as kings and queens, and to rule apart from God's sovereign intervention, even if we are trying to do good things. The idea of self-defense, in turn, can be deformed into an angry, vigilante type of justice, where people fantasize about killing would-be assailants and the like. This does not honor God; we are called to be peacemakers and to pray for our enemies. So again, in obeying God, we see that we are forced into a narrow path where we avoid wrath and violence against those who oppose us on the one side, and a pacifism or apathy that gives into evil on the other hand. Either extreme, incidentally, encourages violence.

Finally, fighting tyranny while also avoiding bloodshed and the chaos of war requires a diligent and consistent engagement in the political arena. To withdraw from politics because it is dirty and full of evil, corrupt actors is to consign the political arena to those very evil, corrupt actors. The only way to faithfully persevere in political action, as an extension of loving one's neighbor, is to operate in the faith and hope promised to us in Scripture—that God will faithfully execute his plan for humankind. We are not home yet, we know that we have an eternal heritage with the Lord. Knowing this, and abiding in it gives us the strength to persevere, even as we love our enemies and take a stand for the truth. This faith is what kept William Wilberforce engaged in the fight against slavery for over forty years and for John Quincy Adams to observe, "Duty is ours, results are God's." All we can do is persist and persevere. Doing so out of a spirit of anger and hatred for one's political enemies will eat us from the inside out.

Meanwhile, we can talk about government overreach all we want, we can talk about burgeoning tyranny and the like, we can decry the evil of elites and bureaucrats, and we can bemoan the destructive actions of radicals. But if that is all we do, we too are guilty of abdicating to tyranny. We were not called to sit on the sidelines. We are called to bring justice to our neighbors and to ensure that our communities are politically, culturally, socially, and above all, spiritually vibrant and healthy. This is what it means to maintain a spirit of covenant and all of the ideas that come with it—*hesed*, mutual accountability, and

---

[14] Amos, 131–132.

noncentralization. This is no easy task, and is essentially a life spent living well, clinging to Christ, working hard, and hoping and praying for the best. We do not judge our actions of love and covenant in the span of just one life; we trust that God is always working, and we trust his own wise, patient timeline. In the end, this is the best way to prevent tyranny—to provide no reason for it to exist, for government to overreach, for monsters to rise up in a vacuum of justice and liberty. Again, duty is ours; results are God's.

Historical Evidence

Many historical events, in which a ruler is forced to change his evil practices or be overthrown, have been based on this same theory of resistance. Events such as the signing of the Magna Carta, the Glorious Revolution the English Bill of Rights, and the American Revolution are excellent examples. In fact, the Declaration of Independence is essentially a covenantal testament that first lays out the biblical foundation of covenant and inalienable rights as the basis for any government and then provides painstaking details about how the king of England and Parliament had time and time again violated the rights of Americans. In essence, these violations equated to a material breach of the covenant. Thus, as Locke postulated, the rulers themselves destroyed the covenant with the people of America, the result being that through the actions of the English, there was a state of war with the American people. And, as the Declaration of Independence closes, there is only one righteous judge upon whom the American people can depend: God himself:

> We, therefore, the Representatives of the united States of America, in General Congress, Assembled, appealing to the Supreme Judge of the world for the rectitude of our intentions, do, in the Name, and by Authority of the good People of these Colonies, solemnly publish and declare, That these United Colonies are, and of Right ought to be Free and Independent States; that they are Absolved from all Allegiance to the British Crown, and that all political connection between them and the State of Great Britain, is and ought to be totally dissolved; and that as Free and Independent States, they have full Power to levy War, conclude Peace, contract Alliances, establish Commerce, and to do all other Acts and Things which Independent States may of right do. And for the support of this Declaration, with a firm reliance on the protection of divine Providence, we mutually pledge to each other our Lives, our Fortunes, and our sacred Honor.

CHAPTER 8
The Culture Wars: The Battle of Ideas in Public Life

Introduction

Worldviews, philosophies, economics, history, and theology—all perspectives, marching into battle like armies, sometimes allies, sometimes mortal enemies. The fighting, both figuratively and literally, is unending and the casualties many. It is fitting that we focus on a discussion of how philosophical, theological, and cultural ideas have waged war against the Gospel message. In many cases, sadly, the institutional churches have themselves been the enemy of the Cross of Jesus Christ. But we also face hostile ideas which in their extremes mutate into Stalinism, radical individualism, and nihilism. In the end, the power of Christ—the good news of the Gospel—is more than sufficient to defeat these enemies, if we cling to Christ. If only we cling to Christ.

Hopefully, the previous chapters have provided some evidence for a Biblical-covenantal approach to life and government, from the interpersonal to the political. Many of the historical examples in the previous chapter have focused on how these biblical principles have been fulfilled in American government. This was not done to portray America as a perfect example of a Christian nation. No nation can claim that, of course. And certainly, America has its own issues with slavery and racism, dealings with Native Americans, and questionable foreign policy goals. But hopefully seeing how these biblical-covenantal ideas manifested in a real political, historical context provides some weight to how things could be. As has always been the case, there continues to be a war on a Christian perspective on life, relationships, and politics. We will conclude with a discussion of these dangers and how a Biblical model encompasses and transcends each of them.

The term *transcend* is used here because each of these perspectives has some vestige of truth hidden in them. A Biblical model acknowledges these truths while rejecting the falsehoods and idols. This discussion will be augmented with references back to the American context from time to time in order to provide some real-world examples. And, in case it needs to be said, I love America. I was born here and lived here all of my life. Part of loving your country is acknowledging its shortcomings. And it is also loving its strengths and being thankful for what makes it unique. One can and should do both without succumbing to some perverse notion of nationalism and idolatry on the one hand or a raging desire to burn it all to the ground and to hate anything with a vestige of American influence. Truly, nuance is needed here, much nuance. And it is always this way with loving America—the same nation that was guilty of so much slavery is the same nation where notions of anti-slavery were first birthed and institutionalized.

Three main threats seek to undermine a Biblical perspective. The first is the worldview of Modernism, or secularism. The second is the worldview of Postmodernism, which claims to reject both Modernism as well as what is perceived to be a stifling Christianity. But the third often confuses the Christian, coming across as a family member when in reality it is nothing more than an enemy of the Gospel. This third enemy is one we have examined before and we will start our discussion with it again, now: Christian legalism.

Christian Legalism: Statism, Racism, and Chauvinism

I promised a constant alignment of all of the topics in this book with what is true at the heart of hearts—at the intrapersonal level where how we see ourselves in Christ, or how we reject God's love and grace through Christ determines everything else. The greatest counterfeit to this Gospel love and adoption is legalism, where we profess a Christian title without relying on the saving work of Christ. We do this in the mistaken notion that we can earn God's favor through our own behavior and above all, in essence become our own gods. This was the original lie given to Adam and Eve (Genesis 3:4-5). As we know, succumbing to the temptation of perfectionism and legalism is easily done, if not simply out of a sense of duty to please God. But this desire quickly shifts into a desire for control which in turn reduces a relationship with the Father to rote duties. This allegedly maximizes our freedom and autonomy, but in reality hollows out our hearts and makes a mockery of intimacy, love, and the joy of abiding in Christ.

When we put performance and the illusion of perfectionism above intimacy with Christ, we see that it impacts the entire culture of our families and relationships with others. If we are leaders of organizations, it can contribute to a toxic culture of perfectionism, workaholism, and a dog-eat-dog mindset that values only economic benefits at the expense of all else. At the State level, this legalism can be seen in fusions of Church and State where private morality is coerced by the State, and in cultures which are heavy on conformance and outward behavior rather than true repentance and obedience to Christ. Often, State-sponsored churches lead to outward conformity only, and with it, projections of man-made righteousness. I suspect that this in turn feeds presumption of racial or gender-based superiority, justifying vile acts at the state level such as racism, slavery, eugenics, and more. After all, if we think we can earn it—either God's favor or some poorly defined sense of superiority and goodness, it is an easy step into thinking that one's culture and people-group are superior to others.

If legalism and perfectionism can damage the culture of an organization, what damage might it do to an entire nation? For instance, the Old South viewed a family's connection to the land and slaves as part of a godly heritage passed down from one generation to the next. Many slave owners saw a divine duty to care for slaves and teach them the Word of God, even though Scripture never affirmed race-based, involuntary, permanent slavery, but rather temporary, voluntary indentured servitude.[1] But this sense of contrived moral superiority perhaps goes back to a sense of the Gospel being subverted in the name of legalism seems to have then led to a false sense of moral and racial superiority.

And of course, we are not just talking about Christian legalism here, but any religion which is works-based and not Christ-based. Any notion of seeking to appease God through good behavior will lead to moralism, legalism, perfectionism, and exploitation of others. It is said that Christianity is the only religion which shows us God pursuing man—God coming to man to save him. Other religious perspectives tell us that we need to get to God, and how to do so; only Christianity tells us that we are incapable of doing so and need divine intervention. Only Christianity shows us God becoming man while not surrendering his divinity, to live among us in this dreary, dusty world and to save us. So, it probably goes without saying that this perspective would reject religions such as Islam. But this text focuses primarily on the Western context. We will see what happens in the future, and whether Islamic perspectives on fusion of Church and State increase.

Meanwhile, the Church has not always reacted well to the secularism of Modernism. Christian fundamentalism arose to fight the onslaught of liberal theology, which attempted to undermine the gospel distinctive in the name of making them more palatable with science and reason. But in doing so, at times it also often created fear, anti-intellectualism, and a withdrawal from society. To the extent that this is true, I would suggest that Christian fundamentalism has morphed into a deformed gospel, and I often use the acronym FAIL to describe its major characteristics:

F: Fear-based—We become so afraid of the advancement of secularism and godlessness in society that we stop trusting God, and unwilling to engage in logical arguments with secularism, much to the chagrin of Christian apologists; also unwilling to engage in the main culture, since society itself is only evil and depraved. In contrast, part of overcoming the arguments of liberal theology, whether it be about the sanctity of Scripture itself, the presence of miracles, the archaeological history of the Bible, or the resurrection is having the faith to believe that the God of the Bible is who he claims to be. If he is the source of all truth and logic, he is also able to guide us in being able to articulate the truth of God's word in a logical manner. This is actually part of having faith. Faith is not the removal of logic. But it does wisely (and logically) reject the folly of putting human reasoning on the throne. If there is no God, there is no human reasoning or even logic. The scientific method cannot exist since all that exists is random chaos. In my own journey of faith, where I have wrestled with difficult and often fair questions from atheists, I have had to overcome my fear and trust that while I might not always know the answers to those questions, I could still trust that God would guide me to find the answers. And He always has. I have never had to shirk away from difficult questions.

A: Authoritarian—This deformation of Christian fundamentalism sees intellectualism and logic as the real enemies (again, Christian apologists everywhere scream in frustration, since

---

[1] Paul Copan, *Is God a Moral Monster? Making Sense of the Old Testament God* (United States: Baker Publishing Group, 2011), 132.

logic is only possible in a God-ordained world). In turn, since we can't seek to engage Scripture logically, and to address critiques of the fundamentals of Scripture in a logically coherent way, the only thing we can do is just believe. This blind faith becomes more about blindly following church leaders, rather than God, who ironically, actually allows us to ask difficult questions and to seek to worship Him with our minds and our intellects. In fact, true, active faith requires the presence of doubt because it is evidence that we are not just blindly obeying, but instead are seeking to understand why we believe what we believe about God and His Word.

I: Isolationist—Again this is manifested by withdrawing from society, withdrawing from the academy, withdrawing from culture because they are all seen as evil and depraved. But we were called to engage all of these as a means of loving God and loving our neighbors.

L: Legalistic—This has already been discussed at great lengths, of course. But I offer it here to show that insofar as this deformed fundamentalism does not allow for thoughtful inquiry and critique, it also likely reduces faith to a set of rules which cannot be questioned because after all, questioning anything leads immediately to liberal theology and secularism. This would include rules about drinking and other forms of entertainment and culture, and usually in prohibitive ways. But an active faith in Christ requires a relationship with God which requires the ability to wrestle with difficult questions, approach cultural engagements in a nuanced, winsome way, and above all to prayerfully rest in God's sustaining grace, rather than simplistic rules, for staying on the straight and narrow way. That is why legalism is often so closely rooted in fear—we are afraid of failing because we have put it all on ourselves to succeed. But the gospel tells us that was never possible. Our only hope is and has always been clinging to Christ.

The problem with fundamentalism is not that it seeks to defend the fundamentals of Scripture, for those fundamentals are the Gospel of Jesus Christ which is our only hope. The problem is when fundamentalism deforms into the attributes listed above. Again, this all derives from putting ourselves on the throne and not God. It is again, natural to be scared about changes in society wherein there is a very real sense of growing darkness and impending doom (this fear, of course, overlooks that the allegedly godlier era of days past also included things such as racism, slavery, and segregation). But it is unacceptable to give into that fear by taking our eyes off of Christ—our active Lord and Savior and high priest, and the Author and Finisher of our faith. That is where the problem lies, as it always has. There will be more on this topic below.

Over-reactions to Over-reactions—the Rise of the Modern Man

As discussed earlier, the version of Church-State fusion in the West occurred during the Middle Ages. It likely informed efforts of colonialization in Asia, Africa, and what is now Latin America. In all of these cases, Christianity was seen as a tool of the State, to reform what were viewed as wayward and depraved cultures in need of heavy-handed reformation. And of course, the Church tried to control the State as well—it was doubtless a bit of both. But the paradigm in which these Church-State struggles occurred had one common theme—that Church and State often exercised the same powers. The skepticism of the Enlightenment, along with eventual developments in science and technology in the era of the Scientific Revolution and Industrial Revolution contributed to a heady confidence in secularism, evolution, and a belief that eventually, science and technology could cure all of mankind's ills. Secularists looked at the superstition of the Catholic Church and the abuse of power which comes with all types of Church-State fusions. Rather than looking at Biblical truths about life and society, and seeing the compatibility of Scripture with science, secularists instead attempted to build a worldview without any divine origin.

Evolution was seen as the hope for improvement, but even evolution requires a fixed point of measurement—indeed, a metaphysical standard of good—to determine that progress has in fact occurred. Even the reliance upon logic requires a metaphysical point of origin; after all, logic is neither a physical entity nor a social construct. If it were a social construct, it could then be changed, and any hope in advancing science would be flimsy and subject to the whims of popular convention.

The Flight to Postmodernism

And besides, science and technology were never enough to cure man. After World Wars I and II and the so-called rational regimes of Stalin and Mao Zedong, the use of science to justify eugenics, the Tuskegee studies, and other atrocities, many argued that Modernism was insufficient, and indeed, highly problematic. Science is just a tool; it is not a sanctifying force. Postmodernism arose, therefore, as an attempt to remedy the extremes of both Modernism and institutional Christianity. To the Postmodernist, the Modernist's arrogance was seen in an over-reliance on Logic, and the one "right way" to order society. This, along with the fusion of Church and State in Western society, led to an unholy alliance where a certain way of life was enforced upon others. It encompassed a belief in the supremacy of the male gender, along with a belief that Western, Christian, white culture was superior to all other ways.

To the Postmodernist, it was this "one right way" that was and is and always has been the cause of hatred, evil, and war. This is why so many people say today that there are no absolutes. Of course, this is a self-contradictory statement. But the reason it is such a popular saying is because of how the worship of science, reason, and technology, which not only contributed to new and devastating ways to kill humans as a tool of one repressive State or another, also contributed to the dehumanization of humans. After all, if there is no spiritual realm, then there we are just matter in motion, cogs in the wheel of nature, and we lack any autonomy or free will, all the easier to use as pawns in warfare or rats in the laboratory. And if these things were not killing people, it was the oppressive regime of Church-State fusion before it.

I am not convinced, meanwhile, that Postmodernism has anything meaningful to say about cultural oppression in general, that is, oppression seen in cultures outside of the West. Too often this worldview seems to focus only on Western oppression and nothing else. But what of other oppressive cultures where women and children are devalued, mutilated, and exploited in numerous ways? And it is often powerless to critique other cultures because of its rejection of absolute truth. Meaning, after all, is only socially constructed, which is to say, that people groups in various cultures create their own meaning and rules of engagement that is culture specific. If we could just stop judging other cultures and respect their own meaning and truth, so the postmodern argument goes, we would have peace and not war, genocide, and other atrocities. But this is flimsy edifice on which to build any moral framework. How can we say that a culture is wrong to exploit women? How can we say that it is wrong for another culture to be so warring? What if a culture does not value human dignity and freedom? Postmodernism tries to assert that individual autonomy is the key and must always be respected. This of course, is a metanarrative—a grand truth—unto itself, which supposedly is frowned upon in Postmodernism. And as for human autonomy, what is to keep a human from saying that his personal truth requires him to exploit others?

So, Postmodernism has sought to embrace space for subjective meaning, feelings, and understandings of life which also allowed for belief in a mysterious, spiritual source of meaning; Postmodernism believes in a God, or many Gods, or a cosmic, universe, god-in-nature, god-in-all-of-us, but never a God or religion who demanded only one way. To the Postmodernist, spirituality is to be preferred over institutionalized religion and formal dogma. It is far better to believe that truth is subjective, or at least that metanarratives should not be trusted, then to repeat the sins of popes and princes who sought to control everyone. Ironically, everything Postmodernism wants to achieve but cannot because it has no foundation for doing so can be achieved through following Christ. Do you want to emphasize the love of one's neighbors, respecting both genders, caring for the poor, and eschewing arrogance and self-righteousness? Then look no further than Jesus Christ himself—our gentle suffering servant. But you must also look on him as the only way, truth, and life. There is no other way. That is the implication of believing in good and evil at all—they may be hard to define at times, but there can only be one, non-mutually exclusive definition, and that definition has to come from a source which was not created and was also sentient, personal and full of love, justice, and beauty. The cry of the Postmodernist is heard and met by our Savior, despite the noise and cacophony of Christian legalism.

Marxism: The Abiding Infatuation

The fact that many secularists and Postmodernists claim some version of Marxism today reveals so much about both worldviews. Marxism has always been a shape-shifter. It has secularist/Modern influences insofar as it arose an attempt to define and solve the problems of injustice with economic explanations and solutions to the problem. It also offered only a structural critique of society—there is no spiritual solution to the problem of evil because man is not spiritual; he is only physical, which is to say he is inseparable from his environment. The only solutions possible, therefore, are structural. In that sense, it was a Modern political ideology. However, it also arose as a reaction to and a rejection of "the Machine" as the Industrial Revolution seemingly destroyed the small family farm and the notion of people controlling and owning their own production. While it may have proffered economic terminology, its lament was always that of the Postmodernist (or historically speaking, the Romanticist), who decried the soul-crushing impact of technology, commerce, and science.

The Culture Wars created a new context for Marxism to emerge as a Postmodern champion of the oppressed. Whereas earlier versions of Marxism focused primarily on how the rich exploited the poor, Postmodern versions, in the forms of critical theory, feminism, queer theory, and multiculturalism, analyzed how cultural norms could be oppressive and could contribute to economic exploitation in very real ways. To the Postmodernist, Marxism was a tool for showing it was not just the rich exploiting the poor; it was the rich, white, Christian heterosexual man exploiting everyone else, especially through cultural norms and expectations (we are again reminded of the dangers of an enculturated, legalistic Christianity). And until people can break free from their "false consciousness" where they see how these often unexamined cultural norms influence them, they will continue to be slaves to the system. Meanwhile, even in the Postmodern version of Marxism, concerns about structuralism continue, as talk of the oppressive patriarchy, white male privilege, etc. abound.

This duality of Marxism does not just speak to its flexibility, but also to the fact that Modernism and Postmodernism are really more similar than different. Both reject the living God, outside of time and space, who created and sustains all things, and communicates an inherent sense of right and wrong (really there is no other philosophical or religious perspective, besides Christianity, which does affirm these things). Thus, both undermine the efficacy of logic and moral reasoning. Both end up explaining our presence via the mysterious existence of the universe; while Postmodernism may attempt to deify the cosmos in keeping with Eastern mysticism, it is merely using different language to describe a closed-system, just as Modernism does. Modernism says that matter was eternal, or that suddenly, matter sprang out of nothing. In both worldviews, any sense of good and evil is subjective. For secularism, self-survival is the only means for determining what is good and evil, and that is highly subjective, just as the Postmodernist would claim.

Meanwhile, to the extent that controversies regarding police brutality and the sexual abuse of women have come to the forefront, many Christians have been concerned about how Marxism has been used as a tool to diagnose the depth of both the abuse of women and minorities. It is appropriate to be concerned about Marxism for the reasons mentioned above, but that should not obviate, on the other hand, the importance of speaking out against such atrocities to the extent they are true. After all, if Christians do not from a Biblical perspective focusing on justice, accountability, and covenant, then it may only be the Marxists who do.

Gospel Implications

There are a couple of major battlefield ideas and conflicts which need further examining as we discuss the Culture Wars. Going too far with either extreme as we wrestle with these ideas is damning. The first is the questions of sexual intimacy and family life, and the second is the question of structural racism.

Sexual Intimacy and Family Life

We should not be surprised that so much of what we disagree about centers around what sexual intimacy should be. The Biblical definition of sexual intimacy is that it occurs exclusively between a man and woman in marriage (Genesis 2:18, 24, Exodus 20:14, Proverbs 5:15-19, Matthew 5:28, Corinthians 7:1-40). The Left in turn argues that this model of sexual intimacy is ultimately an attempt of men to control women, which is why Christians supposedly believe that homosexuality is a sin: because it undermines chauvinism. Further, any attempt to denote gender distinctions is another ploy to infer the inferiority of women and the natural, God-given right of men to rule. And yes, religion—especially Christianity—is seen as a significant part of the problem. Just as in ancient times, religion encouraged the use—and abuse—of women as temple prostitutes, but today, Christianity has become the major religion of the West, and it is the main culprit in perpetuating chauvinism. In turn, the family, led by the man, is seen as the breeding ground for this chauvinism and exploitation, for it is in the family that girls are trained to submit and to believe that they are inferior (submission always implies inferiority), and boys are trained to believe they are superior and should rule. In turn, any women who supports this is guilty of being trapped in false consciousness at best, and seeking their own sliver of power and prestige at worst—especially white women.

To these problems, the Left posits several solutions. First sexual intimacy should be delinked from marriage, and marriage should be delinked from any notion of male-female gender specificity. Sexual expression, moreover, should certainly not be gender-specific. And finally, the institution of the family itself should be radically restructured, possibly to more of a village-commune model so that there can never be any implication that men own or control women and children. What then does Scripture say of these things, and why? Three general themes come to mind.

First, gender specificity in Scripture should never be taken to imply inferiority of women. Men and women are coequal inheritors of God's grace (Genesis 1:27, Galatians 3:28) and are to love and care for one another in marriage (Ephesians 5:33). When the woman is introduced as Adam's helper in Genesis 2:18, the Hebrew word is *ezer*, which was used to depict God as our helper—hardly a position of inferiority! Yes, men are called to lead their marriage, but only as Christ loved the Church sacrificially (Ephesians 5:25). And none of this obviates the need for husbands to submit to their wives (Ephesians 5:21), as any wise husband will tell you, nor does it imply that men should lead all women in all contexts. Further, in the Proverbs 31 portrait of the ideal wife, the wife plays an active role in leading and caring for her family—her husband trusts and respects her implicitly—and she even makes major financial, real estate decisions, and that without even needing to run off to her husband to help her count or grasp business concepts! Again, her husband trusts her. Finally, remember that Christ rebuked the legalism of his time. Note how he respected, befriended, and ministered to and with women (Luke 7:12-13, 8:1-3, 8:43-48, 13:16, John 2:1-12, 4:7-26, 8:10-11) and even revealed his resurrection first to some of these women (Matthew 28), despite the fact that Jewish culture did not trust women to even testify in court.

Second, the Bible does seem to clearly reject homosexuality, from the book of Genesis, where the model for marriage and sexual intimacy is between a man and woman (Genesis 2:24), to the Mosaic law, where it is forbidden (Leviticus 18:22, 20:13), to Christ, who specifically affirms the traditional model of marriage as noted in Genesis (Mark 10:6-9), and finally to the Epistles where it again is prohibited (Romans 1:18-32, 1 Corinthians 6:9-11, 1 Timothy 1:8-10, Jude 7). What then are we to say to those who struggle with same sex attraction or who are confused about their gender? Both of these struggles seem to be related and have caused much pain and confusion for some, who, if they could choose, would prefer to not struggle with these issues at all, especially when living in a culture which for so long as treated them with such scorn and hatred. I will speak more to this below.

Finally, there seems to be something unique about the male and female genders, insofar as they point to the unique relationship of Christ and Church. If Christ is likened to the husband, and the woman is likened to the church (Ephesians 5), it is no surprise that the enemy would seek to destroy gender distinctions, or mire it chauvinism, just as he would seek to destroy sexual intimacy, which is a picture of the love and intimacy of Christ to his church. Further, it is true that the family can be an incubator for abuse and chauvinism, and it is tragic when this happens. But the family is also the only place for a child to be uniquely loved, sheltered, nourished, and cherished. The family unit can and should be an incubator for being introduced to God's wonderful love for his children. I can certainly say that I have better experienced God's love for me as I have discovered how much I love my own children. And I will respectfully push back on anyone who thinks some member of my village or community can love my children more than me or my wife—do not relegate my family to some textbook idea of community life.

Of note too is an alarming trend, ostensibly in the name of subverting the patriarchy, of pushing for sexual rights and so-called freedom to younger and younger ages of children. With great fear and trembling, I will gently submit to the reader that age of consent for children is and will be linked to notions of sexual freedom, gender fluidity, and personal autonomy. It assumes that children can and should have the right to determine their own age of consent and to determine if and when they want to have sex, and with whom. This argument seems to overlook any reality of a child not having the emotional maturity or self-awareness to even make such a decision. In turn, if children do not have the wherewithal to truly make an informed decision, then such ideas about sexual rights and flexible age of consent will only enable predators to have a more active—and perhaps even celebrated—role in encouraging children to engage in sexual activity. In this case, the much-celebrated model of village and community as the true family certainly could be seen to undermine the role of parents in protecting their children from such predatory behavior. And tragically, neither Modernism nor Postmodernism can offer any moral defense against such ideas. For if "matter in motion" is the ultimate reality, as Modernism and secularism argue, then so are concepts like gender and age of consent. And if personal autonomy is supreme, and notions like gender and age of consent are merely culturally contrived norms created by a chauvinistic patriarchy to oppress others, as Postmodernism argues, then why not challenge and even upturn those reified notions?

But to completely address these questions and challenges, let me speak personally to those struggling with same sex attraction or gender confusion.

First, I see you and I see your pain. You are fearfully and wonderfully made. Yes, you struggle with sin, but we all do—we are all confounded by it. You are not unique in that regard, nor should you be scorned or hated for your struggles whether it is same sex attraction or gender confusion or anything else. Yes, sexual sin seems to have a greater impact on our heart and souls, just as sexual temptation seems to be so great because we are trying to somehow capture the love and intimacy God promises for us in him alone and through him alone. There is no other way to be made whole, despite the great lie of sexual temptation. If Scripture is in fact in opposition to same sex attraction, it is even more so in favor of the saving work of Christ in your life, and in my life, and so we can and should cling to Christ together. You need not hide your struggles in the church—you are a welcomed co-survivor of sin and orphanhood, just as you are a welcomed co-laborer in Christ. Whatever you give up for Christ, you will gain much more in return. That is the promise of Scripture to all of us. If you struggle with gender confusion, again, you are fearfully and wonderfully made, just as you are. You can be made whole in Christ, just as I can. Being uniquely a man, or uniquely a woman, will not free you from the pain of life, the slavery of sin, or the striving of the rebel-orphan slave, but being a child of God through Christ can and will free you. I love you, and you are loved, more importantly, by your heavenly Father, intimately and dearly. Do you trust how God has made you, just as you are? You can because he loves you, which you know because you know that he sent Christ to earth to come looking for you.

Whatever else and however else we must discuss these issues—and we must—this note of love to all who are lost can never be ignored and this is the hope—the only true hope—that any of us have.

Privilege and Racism

One theme from the Culture Wars is the idea of structural racism, and the notion of white male privilege in particular. This idea essentially argues that white people—and men in particular—are inherently racist and inherently devalue and resist the upward mobility of minorities, for fear of losing out on wealth, power, and control. White women, meanwhile, are often guilty of racism, even though they are victims of chauvinism, as discussed above. In this context, white women are cooperating with the enemy for some semblance of prestige and standing, rather than identifying with other minorities to overturn the patriarchy. This argument assumes that essentially, Western culture is inherently racist and predicated on the abuse and exploitation of minorities through slavery and colonization. How would the Gospel speak to these claims? We will find that it is a very nuanced answer.

First, we should never be surprised that one culture exploits another. That is simply a common fact of human existence which Scripture, time and time again, critiques. So yes, white Christians should be quick to examine and act against any type of exploitation as it occurs. We should not pretend that silence on these issues of structural injustice is appropriate because we are focused on preaching the Gospel rather than politics—would it be acceptable to see our neighbor being murdered or raped but to walk on by, claiming that were late to church? Just because an issue has a political dimension does not mean that we should ignore it, or else we should also ignore travesties such as sex trafficking and abortion.

Further, we should not be afraid to examine any implicit racism in our own hearts. As Proverbs 9:8 (ESV) warns: "Do not reprove a scoffer, or he will hate you; reprove a wise man, and he will love you"—we should appreciate anyone helping us to see potential sin, especially because sin is so pervasive and often hard to discern. We are not the most objective judges of our own hearts, after all. And remember that we are called to not be conformed to the ways and culture of this world, with all of its greed, materialism, and apathy (Romans 12:1-2). Also, our disposition as humans is that of entitlement, pride, and self-sufficiency, correct? So to the extent Western culture has perpetuated racism, and to the extent that we are always waging a war against being imprinted upon by our erstwhile culture which loves ease and pleasure at the expense of covenantal love of our neighbor and self-government, we must always, always be on guard.

But most swords are double-sided and cut both ways. For those eager to point out the sin of white male privilege, first, thank you, and second, remember that the Gospel cuts far deeper and more comprehensively than merely focusing on white male privilege. We are all exposed before the righteous judge, and one way we are found guilty is in our urge to self-righteously condemn others. We do love to sit in the judgement seat reserved alone for the righteous Judge. To automatically assume that all white people are guilty of implicit racism is to claim to know the heart of man . . . which again belongs solely to the domain of the omniscient God and not mere mortals (also it is racist, but that is another matter). If we are going to speak about implicit biases and the like, and we absolutely should, then let us also speak about how delicious it is to judge and berate others—we are highly addicted to it, and then we are enslaved by it (James 1:13-15).

Finally, this talk of structural racism and injustice, specifically from those on the Left, tends to lead to a sweeping disqualification of anything that is seen as "white" or "Western." The previous chapter spent a great deal of time detailing progress and advancement which absolutely should not be dismissed or ignored. Dear friends, we only have what we have; it is always the best of times and simultaneously the worst of times. We are always trying to reclaim what we can that is good while simultaneously trying to swim safely to the shore from the shipwreck of human existence. Should we throw away a life raft because we lifted it off the slave ship in our escape? There is indeed one who wants to see everything burn down, who wants to see every good thing perish—should we join him in his revels as human society disintegrates? Or should we cling to Christ, and seek to be about his business—loving others (including white people) and recognizing that if God can change our evil hearts, and work despite our frailty, that he can and always has worked throughout human history, despite the worst of human evils? Will we deny his good work in society and culture in the name of identifying evil?

As an aside, this is why I cannot decry the American experiment with democracy. I agree with Frederick Douglass, who saw the Declaration of Independence as a pro-freedom democracy. And even though the Constitution did not end slavery, neither did it even mention the term, for fear that it would institutionalize the concept. The two-thirds provision in slavery, which only counted slaves as two-thirds of a person, was not meant to dehumanize them but rather to limit the political influence of the Southern states, who simultaneously wanted to deprive slaves of their liberty on the one hand but on other hand wanted to count them as full persons—but only for the sake of increasing Southern representation in Congress (no thank you). Those founders opposed to slavery had to choose between solidifying a working union which could withstand foreign influence and tyranny or ending any union. They chose to solidify the union with the hope that slavery was on the decline. As soon as stipulated in the Constitution they ended the slave trade. Further, breaking apart the union may have actually furthered slavery, as likely foreign nations would have had greater access to western territories in America, and would have brought slavery with them, just as southern states would have as they set up new territories in the West. Meanwhile, slavery would have continued in the South without any influence from northern abolitionists. The point here is that there are no easy answers. By all means speak out against evils such as slavery, racism, and yes the exploitation of Native Americans. But do not, in turn, destroy documents and institutions of government which uniquely demonstrated covenantal principles of government. Always reclaim and preserve what you can for the good of your neighbor while fighting—always fighting—the evil that remains.

The Impacts of False Gods

Modernism and Postmodernism both offer failed outcomes. Since this book proposes to start with the intrapersonal and move outward, we can do the same with both of these worldviews. Both Modernism and Postmodernism start with the foundational presupposition that the universe is all there is. Technically, Postmodernism attempts to spiritualize the cosmos with ideas that "God is in all of us" and "God is in everything". A Christian knows that these precepts are to some extent true, but the Godhead is also independent of time and space is also personal and intimate. A spiritualized cosmos, a "force" within all of us, a deified nature—none of these suggest personhood, sentience, or the ability to communicate truth and meaning. In either case, whether going the route of Modernism or Postmodernism, all one is left with is an impersonal, non-sentient force and matter in motion. Thus, there is no inherent meaning, no true beauty, love, or justice, no ultimate, eternal significance. Even personal sentience is an illusion—we "think" we are thinking, but we are just a product of physical processes, matter-in-motion. Or, in the Postmodern view, our meaning is only for us. We cannot say that what is true for us is true for someone else. The great mystery that is supposed to comfort us—the great "other," the oneness with the cosmos that is supposed to free us from personal pain and suffering—also denies the importance of being an individual at all.

In turn, it is no surprise that the Modernism-Postmodernism matrix leads to gender confusion. If matter is in constant motion, or if meaning is entirely subjective, then the very essence of who we are as men and women is open for debate. The Biblical perspective says otherwise—male and female were both made in God's image (Genesis 1:26), so those gender distinctions are obviously holy. Woman was created to be a helper, but not in a subordinate, inferior way at all. The Hebrew found there connotes that a woman helps her husband similar to how God helps man. The submission of a wife to her husband, further, comes within the context of mutual submission (Ephesians 5:21), and is a picture of how Christ pursues the Church. This is a holy, mutual submission, just as there is holy, mutual submission within the Trinity.

But it is also a submission which is seen in marriage only, and does not imply submission of every woman to every man. Further, while it appears that elders are called to be men (1 Timothy 3:1-7, Titus 1:5-9), this still allows for women to have an active role in church leadership, particularly once we understand that leadership is not just positional but also about influence. Assuming this traditional interpretation is correct, it seems to suggest that there is a connection between submission in marriage and the submission of the Church to Christ as Ephesians 5:24-25 suggests. But what it does *not* suggest is an inherent sense that women are inferior to men, or that men should always be in all formal positions of leadership in any type of organization in society. Further, we are reminded again of the mutual submission of the members of the Trinity, none of whom are inferior to one another.

Christian legalism, Modernism or Postmodernism—these are all false gods and the worship of whom results in bitter and empty ends. In all of these, there exists an inherent haughtiness. Putting man on the throne is the original sin conceived in the Garden, and so it is not unique to any of these but each has a slightly unique manifestation. For Modernism, it is found in the old Renaissance-humanist assertion that "man is the measure of all things," rather than God. For Postmodernism, it is found in every person making meaning and truth for themselves, as if there lived experiences, cultural influences, and personal opinions were sufficient to attain true goodness. It can also be seen in Christian legalism, since again, humans are trying to earn their own salvation and sanctification. In any case, it can contribute to a petulant self-sufficiency, which sneers at the needs of others and boasts in its own strength. This can come wrapped in the political ideology of conservatism, but it is not, in fact, conservatism. While conservatism favors limited government, it does not do so not to give the individual unlimited power, but rather because a principal presupposition of conservatism that within the confines of every human heart lies a tyrant, raging for control without obedience to God, moral law, or care for others. This tyrant boasts in his own strength and looks down upon the perceived weaknesses of others. There is no regard for covenantal bonds with neighbors, the community, or the poor. To the poor, the tyrant says, "work harder"; to the rich, the tyrant looks on with greed, envy, and avarice. This is not conservatism—it is simply selfishness and greed.

The Gospel and Covenant vs. the Isms

And still, there is only one Hope who provides truth, meaning, and healing to the world. Remember that Jesus Christ rejected the legalism and racism of his day—he railed against the hypocrisy of the Pharisees. He loved and ministered to the Samaritans, when the Jews would only hate them (and the Samaritans would only hate the Jews) (John 4:1-42). He represented an objective starting point for meaning, love, and values that have always existed, even before the creation of time itself and the universe. He was the Divine *logos* and by coming into this world of suffering and frailty as fully God and fully man, He affirmed both logic, as the living Word of God, as well as the inherent value of all human beings.

His complete and final work on the cross provides a searing white fire that burns away the dross of all forms of religious legalism. His words and saving power which changed hearts and upended entire empires provides a thoughtful warning to both the radicals of the Left who want to upend all structures, from the family to the State, and hard right authoritarians who think that brute force should be used to beat down the radicals, or that nationalism is our hope. Both stand in judgement, along with the legalist, and all must seek salvation as frail and needy children in need of forgiveness and adoption. And He is not one for hubris, for haughty rebukes, for impassioned diatribes. His words were gentle and yet enough to both overwhelm his captors in the garden and pronounce the final doom of hopelessness and despair: "It is finished" (John 19:28-30).

In accepting the Gospel of Christ, we do not reject concerns about structural injustice or the dangers of ingrained legalism. But we understand that external, structural changes have to be balanced with internal, heart-level changes. Covenant affords us the means to both: it reminds us that we are humans living in close contact with one another, with mutual obligations to care and support one another. This requires intimacy, especially since most societal ills are caused by broken homes, where children learn to act as orphans rather than self-governing individuals who know they are loved.

While a Marxist approach would seek to radically restructure or remove the family unit, the Gospel would seek instead to heal broken hearts, so that mothers and fathers learn to love one another and their children. While a secularist/Postmodern perspective would seek to undermine gender distinctions because it is believed that such distinctions convey inferiority of women, a Gospel-centered perspective would say that we are male and females, equally made in God's image, and equally sharing in God's glory and eternal inheritance (Galatians 3:28). A covenantal perspective also reminds us that part of loving our neighbor means addressing those structural injustices.

Sometimes that is the work of churches, families, communities, non-profits, and individuals. This is in keeping with the covenantal notion of noncentralization and federalism, which call for a multi-sphered approach to societal issues, as opposed to statism. But sometimes, when inalienable rights are being violated, the State must step in and restrain those evils. Even so, this should not occur absent the involvement of other spheres of society. The State can only restrain evil; the Church acting in the power of the Gospel as opposed to empty legalism and moralism, can be the Spirit's agent for change and reform—not just of structures, but of the eternal hearts and souls of frail and broken human beings.

This is true even at the foreign policy level. No State or regime can seek to make another people group or nation good. This is and always has been the role of the Christ's Church—the power of God working in human vessels despite our frailty. The Stalinists have forgotten this (or never knew it) and a so-called Christian America likely has been led astray in attempts to force democracy in other parts of the world—an extension of the notion of Manifest Destiny—where it first requires the work of the Gospel to change hearts.

Meanwhile, the Culture Wars rage on, buildings burn, judgments are uttered in the arenas of social media. We are quick to judge, quick to anger, slow to run back to our loving Father who truly has the right to judge but instead showed mercy. We rightly decry past sins such as racism and chauvinism—symptoms of a legalist culture, but now we seem more comfortable with a host of sexual sins and rampant individuality—symptoms of a licentious, promiscuous culture—which also debase the human heart and soul. If ever there were a time for a thoughtful exposition of how the Gospel walks the narrow way between stumbling legalism and raging radicalism, the time is now.

CHAPTER 9
Where Angels Fear to Tread—Thoughts on Public Policy

Thus far in this book, we have discussed how principles related to adoption in Christ and covenant can and should impact everything from matters of the heart all the way to government structure and processes. This has been quite an expansive journey and one that is almost over. But before we are quite finished, let us press our luck to discuss yet one more expansive topic—public policy—using the same approach for every other chapter. For men and women who want to serve the Lord in the public arena, or who are involved in realms of society impacted by laws and regulations, or just citizens who want to know how to vote, it is always helpful to have some guiding thoughts.

Public policy defines first and foremost the laws passed by a government, and secondarily, the regulations created to enact those laws. In the American context, it seems that many people focus only ensuring that their favored political party is able to pass a law with little emphasis on how those laws are regulated and executed. Public administrators have some leeway in filling in the gaps where vague laws need specific regulations. Beyond this complexity, there are other reasons that the study of public policy is subject to much disagreement and dispute. Often competing sides do not agree on the nature of the policy problem, much less policy solutions. This is due again to human frailty, informed not just by personality differences as discussed previously, but also worldview and ideological differences. Thus, every policy debate has theological, political, ideological, economic, historical, and cultural facets. Trying to ascertain all of these influences can feel like diagramming a flame. But below we will discuss at least some guiding themes which should help bring at least some clarity.

Rebels and the Power of Elites

In America's political system, where the Culture Wars have been raging steadfastly since the 1960s, it is easy for one side to decry the threats and exploitation of "big business" and the other side to decry the threats of "big government." It is not quite that simple, because when people forget the inheritance they could have in Christ, and instead rebel against both his law and his love, they seek to accumulate power to themselves. From the dawn of time, the rich and powerful have always sought to game the system for their benefit. It is no surprise that verses like Isaiah 10:1-2 condemn this very behavior and it is no surprise that public policy often favors the rich and powerful. This assessment was not meant for merely cursing the darkness. Everyone can complain about this unholy alliance of the rich and powerful, and indeed, the Marxists have done so to the point of fine art. What we want to do, however, is add to our statecraft and public policy analysis an understanding of how often regulations and laws favor the rich and powerful.

Regulations That Favor the Powerful at the Expense of Competition

First, regulations often limit competition so that more established businesses can rest easier in the marketplace. It will be argued here that the free market is a good biblical model for economic activity. It favors private property, but within the context of using that property to bring value to the consumer. Certainly, an incessant desire to grow, conquer, and develop can lead to environmental and economic exploitation, but that is the problem of greed, not the free market. The free market is no place to rest easy; a successful business model leads to imitators seeking to profit in the same way. Businesses are forced to grow and adapt, and to be quick to respond to customer concerns and changing developments. In fact, the idea of *creative destruction* refers to how a new business model, service or product is so popular and new that it dramatically undermines established goods, services, and ways of doing business.

No established business likes to be on the receiving end of such creative destruction, and in fact, most start-ups do not make it past five years of existence, so even without such innovation, it is hard to succeed in the free market. We know that God gave Adam and Eve work to do, even before the Fall, so in turn, we know that work exists has part of the perfect, created order. Work is now difficult, but it is still inherent to the *imago dei* each of us possess. To survive economically, we must work hard and with integrity, and trust that God alone is our provider. He does not promise us incredible prosperity, but he does promise to meet our needs (Psalm 37:25).

Time and time again, Scripture warns about the dangers of greed. The rich boast in their riches only to see wealth sprout wings and fly away (Proverbs 3:25); the wicked plot violence for wealth and often find themselves trapped in their own snares (Psalm 141:10, Proverbs 5:22); Christ mocked the rick ruler who sought to be so wealthy that he would never need to work (Luke 12:13-21) and above all, Scripture warns that the love of money is the root of all evil (1 Timothy 6:10). The problem here is not money or private property, but rather seeking emotional and spiritual security and refuge in wealth. We seek a life of wealth and ease in this life because we fear death and decay; but God would have us accept that in Him not only will our material needs be met but more importantly our eternal, spiritual needs will be met as well. We were not placed *in* this life to simply *for* this life; we were placed in this life to find our ways toward our Creator and Father in Christ, and to recognize our eternal inheritance.

To achieve that hope in us, he does not desire a life of ease and wealth for us, so some of us may indeed be wealthy, but rather a life of hard work, and yes, often suffering, so that we would learn to trust him. Everyone will suffer in this life, but the suffering of the righteous is not that of rebel-orphan-slaves who find themselves caught on the crooked trail of wickedness, beset by wild animals, blinded by the darkness of sin, as Proverbs so aptly describe. The sufferings of the sinful are those whose hearts are still controlled by the abiding chaos of sinful desires—the screeches and howls of unmet and never satisfied wants and striving. The suffering, hard work, and trials God intends for His children is to free us from those desires and cravings; in effect to free us from the slavery of sin.

However, when the rich reject what could be their eternal inheritance, and instead use their wealth and influence to lobby lawmakers to create laws that favor their businesses at the expense of others, they are guilty of undermining the free market. This is known as rent-seeking and crony capitalism. Often regulations are introduced as a means of safety and standardization, but only the more established businesses can afford to successfully meet those standards, and smaller businesses and entrepreneurs cannot compete. Thus a new oligarchy of elites and experts are created who do not favor the so-called commoners who might have good ideas but cannot suffer the regulatory burdens created through crony capitalism. This is not to say that there is never a need for such regulations, for greed and laziness can certainly lead to callous business practices that can hurt others and the environment. But regulations seem to breed more regulations, and camels are eventually undone by the final straw that breaks their back. So it is with excessive regulations.

Economic Planning That Protects Greed

Meanwhile, another type of lawmaking also protects this oligarchy of the rich and powerful. Chasing after money can consume the soul; like any addictive behavior it leads to excessive risk taking and essentially gambling. Whereas Scripture urges us to work hard, bring value to our customers and neighbors and trust in God's provision with a heart of contentment and joy, the slaves to greed must always find new and faster ways to make money, hand-over-fist. The world's oligarchy of risk takers are beset with this desire—are indeed slaves to it. The rules and laws of finance favor borrowing money in the hopes of high (and hopefully fast) profit.

The financing laws of modern nations seem to favor this behavior in the name of economic development. Credit and borrowing are cheap, and since having national currency linked to a gold standard is no longer in vogue, money can be printed endlessly. In cases such as this, where money-chasing is falsely equated with economic development, the stock market may reveal high growth, but the marketplace may not reflect much in the way of increases in employment or productivity of goods and services. To the extent that this observation is true, it reveals a corruption of profit, where externally, there are signs of wealth and prosperity, but at its core, it is rotten and without merit.

This is the fruit of endless, impatient greed, but there is an even more bitter harvest, for eventually this cycle of money-chasing catches up with the slaves of greed; eventually, the good times end and the guilty find themselves upside down in enormous debt with little in the way of assets to show for it. When smaller businesses make such a mistake, they end up paying for it with bankruptcy or termination of their business. But when the oligarchy finds itself in such a situation, the State, which of course is often beholden to the oligarchy, effects an enormous bailout, fueled by the taxes of its people and more money-printing to supposedly save the economy. But often the only people saved are the rich and powerful, while the poor and middle-class see little benefits, especially since the original round of money-making was not producing jobs or economic development anyway.

Orphanhood and Idolizing the State

Part of the reason such egregious policy-making occurs is because people who should have put their hope in God alone, and in turn, received the gift of self-government, instead abandon that hope. As a result, they are quick to idolize the State and gift it the absolute sovereignty that only belongs to God as discussed in Chapter 6:

Who Is Sovereign?		
The Individual	God	**The State**
Anarchy	Liberty/Self-government	**Tyranny**

One manifestation of this is an expectation that the State can manage, plan, and control the economy. Many are the economic theories that propose wise management of the economy, precisely to control the excessive growth and hype discussed above which in turn lead to often severe economic downturns. Again, the real problem is people, beholden to greed, chasing profit and ease. Good growth for a business can lead to this greed, fueled by a lazy assumption that the good times will always be there. But a wise person knows that life always has ups and downs, summers and winters, life and death. During the good times, one should live and plan for the bad times. As the book of Ecclesiastes so eloquently warns us, God does not promise us tomorrow (6:1-12, 9:1-12, 7), and we should not seek to live a life of frivolity and ease (5:8-20; 7:2).

The State cannot really prevent this heart problem. Even if it seeks to use a central monetary agency to control economic growth through tax and spending and regulating the flow of money in the economy, it will find that while it may seek to control the irrational behavior of the people, it will never be able to control the irrational behavior of the very lawmakers who control the spending and printing of money, especially since the power to tax and spend is the power to gain favor with the rich and powerful. "Rational" theories of economic behavior do not survive contact with the irrational human heart and having power as a lawmaker does not tame that irrationalism, but often only enables it. Further, efforts to centralize the economy, in the name of taming it, often serves to make it easier for human frailty to infect the entire system.

Slavery: Regulations That Undermine Self-Government

And when the State is given the power to centralize and control the economy, it also has the power to enslave. Part of being enslaved is being shielded from one's own mistakes. Part of being enslaved is being spared the need to work and grow, and to learn the value of hard work. When the State seeks to offer welfare to the poor, the best intentions to care for the poor can backfire and actually encourage laziness. This is not to say that the poor are always lazy—far from it. Hardships befall good and honest people, and the mistakes of past generations roll downhill and accumulate speed from one generation to the next as the impacts accrue. The concern here is that welfare can make those impacts worse, rather than helping them. The path of prosperity is the path of self-government: hard work, education, and if one has a family, completing one's education before there are children.

Even Christians might balk at this commentary—especially those from a more liberal political perspective. They would argue that the Bible is clear that we are to help the poor, and they are right. But in our discussions of the sin–crime distinction from Chapter 5, along with the related discussion of the dual roles of Church and State, we can infer that the Church is called to provide more direct and intimate support and care of the poor, which includes a relationship with those people that goes well beyond that which a civil bureaucrat can provide. This relationship includes loving accountability so that financial support can be measured against a demonstration of self-government and growth. Social workers cannot speak to the spiritual side of poverty, and often cannot have the relational collateral to truly measure whether a person is taking the needed steps to grow.

Nothing is easy about any of this, of course, but often state interventions are an attempt to pretend that they are—that financial support, education, and job training will be sufficient for most people. It will certainly be sufficient for some, happily, but there is also a good body of research showing that welfare has caused entire generations to lose ground in the fight against poverty and even systemic racism. Aid to the poor is also problematic in the foreign arena as well. When foreign aid squelches local business development (especially when it becomes the target of corrupt politicians in the host nation), it actually undermines the self-government of the very people-group it is trying to help.

Even the State's intervention in education can be have this impact. College education is seen as a major path for prosperity, and in the past it has been in part because it was not as common as it is today. But when the State tries to provide funding for the poor to attend college, as well as financing loans for the middle class, it suddenly makes it easier for everyone to go to college, which in turn makes it an expectation for everyone to go to college. So now graduates are encumbered with school loans and unable to find jobs as easily because there are so many of their own kind also looking for jobs. Education is a difficult enough task for the State simply because one cannot truly educate without talking about the meaning of life and the nature of truth and values. These domains inherently touch upon matters of religion and worldview. When secular states seek to ignore the religious and philosophical implications of education in the name of "separation of Church and State" it undermines the very usefulness of education and does so with the inherently coercive power of the State.

Meanwhile, regulations for energy and environmental safety can also serve to negatively impact those arenas. The State, at its highest level, definitely has a divine mandate in preventing environmental damage, as this problem directly threatens inalienable rights and the safety of future generations. But again, excessive regulations can stymie energy development. In some cases, in the American context, restrictions on domestic development of energy only means that America is buying oil from nations with even less environmental regulations. Regulations for nuclear energy, which is a clean source of energy, have consistently hindered the development nuclear energy as a reliable source of energy for America over the course of many decades.

Reformation, Not Revolution; Substance, Not Structuralism

So then what is the State, or the people, more generally speaking, to do if they are to address structural injustice? One might think that the above commentary denies the existence of injustice or seeks to downplay every evidence of suffering simply to poor life choices of those who suffer. On the contrary, real suffering does exist. It does in fact often occur at the behest of the rich and powerful, thanks to evils like crony capitalism and rent-seeking.

Yes, the State does have a role in caring for the poor but if we again assume the sin–crime distinction as a guide, then its role in caring for the poor falls in the domain of preventing and punishing harm to consumers and corruption while the Church seeks to deal with the connection between spiritual and economic poverty through interpersonal relationships and the accountability that comes with it. Case in point: The Civil Rights era in America lead to great advancement for African Americans, because the State was dealing with the structural injustice of racism and the related violation of inalienable rights. Addressing those injustices did not inherently or directly improve the economic status of African Americans, but it did create the context for them to demonstrate their own self-government and advance economically and socially. But when Great Society legislation sought to deal with their economic status, one generation of African Americans actually lost ground for reasons discussed above.[1]

Does this approach alone guarantee the removal of poverty and injustice? Hardly. But it is folly to think that the State can be the one to end injustice once and for all. That is the hope of many who reject Christ's warning that there will always be poverty (Mark 14:7). There will always be poverty because there will always be free will and in turn there will always be evil. The State can and should do its part to fight evil and injustice, particularly in the realm of the violation of inalienable rights and preventing rent-seeking and corruption, just as the Church should focus on its domain and seeking to address the spiritual and material needs of people who are willing to be helped.

The Marxist and other radicals will find all of this to be weak sauce indeed. While we talk about the dangers of crony capitalism and rent seeking, they would instead point to the problems private property itself and any system (structure) that would continue to perpetuate the exploitation of the poor. While we talk about how the best chances of avoiding a life of emotional instability, poverty, and crime is being raised in a traditional family by loving parents, many on the far left seek the abolition of the very family itself since it allegedly perpetuates

---

[1] See Charles Murray, *Losing Ground* and Thomas Sowell's *Vision of the Anointed*. Obviously, this is a highly debated topic. I do not mean to gloss over that. But I think this would be the primary concerns about social welfare programs—that they don't actually alleviate poverty, but rather exacerbate the problem.

chauvinism and further abuses just as capitalism allegedly perpetuates the abuse of the rich over the poor along with other vile practices such as racism and even environmental damage.

To Marxists and other radicals, there is no spiritual component to evil because there is no God or spiritual domain at all. If there is no metaphysical presence, there is no metaphysical solution and we are all the product of a physical environment. The only solution, then, is to radically abolish the structures of evil themselves. But while revolutionary zeal may be a fire which burns well, it does not do much for rebuilding and recrafting a new Eden. Just as Marx has been criticized for having very little in the way of having a specific blueprint for the future, so does any attempt at radical revolution always fail because it can only remove structures. And while it attempts this removal, it can perpetuate an incredible loss of life and suffering as the case of Lenin, Stalin, Mao Tso Tung, and other Marxist dictators so tragically demonstrate. Replace one structure with new structures, and the problem of evil will still remain because first and foremost, it is a deeply human, spiritual, and intrapersonal problem. The curse of the rebel-orphan-slave persists above and beyond any type of structural solution.

Covenant and Tools for Sound Policy

But there is and always will be a need for structural reform. The covenantal notion of non-centralization is one such structural reform as it ensures that power is disseminated and overlapping. It does not promise efficiency, only effectiveness at lessening the tyrannical impulse to amass and centralize power. A true Marxist, would at the very least, appreciate the grassroots, community based flavor of this structural approach, but so should true conservatives. When the State acts within its domain, which is to ensure justice by preventing rent-seeking and economic statism, and protect inalienable rights—including those of the unborn—hopefully the Church can strengthen its role as the salt. And this is minimally, where you come in. Are you a mother? A father? A son or daughter? Love your neighbors, love your church. Preach the Gospel. Seek political reform. Remember that with great Christian revivals comes political change and reform—not bloody revolutions, but thoughtful reforms based on the consent of the people via their elected officials. If you are a parent, love your spouse and your children and do not let your career or hobbies distract you from your main calling. Save them from the path of the rebel-orphan-slave. Save yourself, by God's grace.

CONCLUSION

A long and expansive book deserves a short ending, if not merely as an expression of gratitude to the long-suffering reader. Finishing a book is a great gift a reader gives to an author, and I am truly grateful that you have made it this far. Below, then, are some final reminders.

Remember how much you are loved by God, how much you are valued, and how you are needed to stand in the gap for your family, your neighbors, your community, your church, your country, and the world, in whatever manner the Lord would have for you.

Remember that in matters of soul and state, "the heart of the matter is a matter of the heart." The Lord changes our hearts and thereby changes the world. We do not always like His slow and patient ways (Ecclesiastes 8), His incessant emphasis on gently leading us to choose to abide in Him. We would rather there be some external, easier means for change and reformation, both for us and our world. But we forget that this so-called external world is not the ultimate reality. The ultimate reality's portal is our hearts, and through that stretches eternity. We would do well to not waste that knowledge.

Remember that the Gospel provides simple truths to understand, but complex truths to live out. Sometimes it seems that the simpler the truth, the more difficult it is to live out. Such is the case with tendencies such as legalism, self-sufficiency, perfectionism, and materialism. The antidote is God's grace through the saving work of Jesus Christ. Truth encompasses all of the facets of our lives, often in overlapping ways, as this book has hopefully demonstrated.

Remember that idolatry and abiding are always in competition with one another for your heart and soul. We are called to abide in Christ. This is the simple and starting truth for a life lived well. I do not prefer this; it is by no means my default, spiritual disposition. I tend to either over-work or over-indulge in diversions. But my time is relative; making time to abide and rest in the Lord never detracts from the work I must do, I have found, and being overly enamored with diversion never gives me true rest (or true productivity). But adultery pulls us away from this singular focus. To adulterate means to weaken with inferior substances. In our case, we so easily adulterate the Gospel with materialism, self-sufficiency, empty intellectualism, and so much more, and thereby we orphan ourselves yet again.

Remember that the joy of the Lord is the best path for fighting evil in this world, whether in your own life or in the greater fights of our times. There is no use for anger and fear. They will only eat you from the inside out and take your eyes off of your loving Lord and Savior.

Remember that yes, being engaged meaningfully with your neighbors, your community, and your world is taxing and above your human capacity to do well. It takes much work to practice the truths discussed in this text. But you are loved dearly, and your gentle Savior offers you His yoke so that you can do all that He has called you to do (1 Thessalonians 5:24).

Finally, and again, just as we started out at the beginning of this book, remember that you are a beloved child of God. You are not alone. Your loving Savior, Jesus Christ, knows you and loves you. He is ever calling you back to Him. That is a truth worthy of concluding a book:

> *When I saw him, I fell at his feet as though dead. But he laid his right hand on me, saying, "Fear not, I am the first and the last, and the living one. I died, and behold I am alive forevermore, and I have the keys of Death and Hades* (Revelation 1:17–18, ESV).

In Christ find your hope and consolation. He is more than sufficient!

REFERENCES

Amos, Gary. *Defending the Declaration*. Charlottesville, VA: Providence Foundation, 1994.

Berman, Harold. *The Origin of the Western Legal Tradition*. Cambridge, England: Harvard University Press, 1983.

Burtness, Bill. *Judah Bible Curriculum: Education for Liberty*. Urbana, IL: Bill Burtness, 1991.

Congar, Yves O.P. *After Nine Hundred Years*. New York: Fordham University Press, 1959.

Conklin, Carli N. *The Pursuit of Happiness in the Founding Era: An Intellectual History*. Columbia, MO: University of Missouri Press, 2019.

Copan, Paul. *Is God a Moral Monster? Making Sense of the Old Testament God*. United States: Baker Publishing Group, 2011.

Eidsmoe, John. *Christianity and the Constitution: The Faith of Our Founding Fathers*. Grand Rapids, MI: Baker Books, 1987.

Elazar, Daniel J. "Covenant as the Basis of the Jewish Political Tradition." *The Jewish Journal of Sociology* 20, (1978): 5.

Elazar, Daniel J. *Covenant & Polity in Biblical Israel*. New Brunswick, NJ: Transaction Publishers, 1995.

Elazar, Daniel J. "The Political Theory of Covenant: Biblical Origins and Modern Developments." *Publius* 10, no. 4 (1980): 3–30.

Elazar, Daniel J. "The Almost-Covenanted Polity." Workshop on Covenant and Politics—Temple University, 1982.

Freeman, Gordon M. "The Dark Side of Covenant." Workshop on Covenant and Politics—Temple University (1980): 1–20.

Harris Laird R., Gleason L. Archer, Jr., and Bruce K. Watke. *Theological Wordbook of the Old Testament*. Volumes 1 & 2. Chicago, IL: The Moody Press, 1980.

Scazzero, Peter. *Emotionally Healthy Spirituality*. Grand Rapids, MI: Zondervan, 2017.

Kamrath, Angela E. *The Miracle of America: The Influence of the Bible on the Founding History and Principles of the United States of America for a People of Every Belief*. Second Edition. Houston, TX: American Heritage Education Foundation, 2014, 2015.

Loizides, Lex. "Religious Legalism and Racism—Frederick Douglass." *Church History Review*. March 21, 2019. https://lexloiz.wordpress.com/2019/03/21/christian-legalism-and-racism-frederick-douglass/.

Mott, Stephen Charles. *A Christian Perspective on Political Thought*. Oxford University Press, 1993.

Tadmor, Naomi. "People of the Covenant and the English Bible." *Transactions of the Royal Historical Society* 22, (2012): 95–110.

Torrance, James B. "The Covenant Concept in Scottish Theology and Politics." Workshop on Covenant and Politics—Temple University, 1980.

Tuck, Richard. *Natural Rights Theories*. New York: Cambridge University Press, 1979.

Waldstein, Michael. "The Spousal Logic of Justification: St. Thomas and Luther on Paul's Key Topic Statement Romans, 1: 17." Doctor Communis 1/2 (2009): 185–197.

Walzer, Michael. *The Revolution of the Saints: A Study in the Origins of Radical Politics*. Cambridge: Harvard University Press, 1965.

INDEX

A

Active dialogue, 53–54, 58
America's Declaration of Independence, 74

B

Between God and man
   authentic leadership, 47–48
   cross of Christ, 47–48
   nature of empowerment, 45–46
   personal attributes of leadership, 44
   selfish empowerment, 46
   servant leadership and following Christ, 46–47
   transformational leadership, 47
   vision-casting, 47
Biblical-covenantal approach, 95
Biblical view, 67

C

Christian America, 108
Christian legalism
   FAIL, 97–98
   God becoming man, 96
   legalism and perfectionism, 96
Christians
   decry political activity, 64
   spring of water welling up to eternal life, 65
Christian Self Government, 61
Church life and conflict
   avoid gossip and slander, 32–33
   church leadership, 32
   conflict resolution, 34
   cynicism and burnout, 31
   side of heaven, 33
   vision for ministry, 33
Church pulpit, 61
Conflict resolution
   dangers of unmet, 30
   inevitable, 30
   opportunity to grow, 31
   personality trait, 29–30
   personal note, 29
   prevents evil, 34
   unifying commonality, 29
   unspoken expectations, 30
Constant tension, 31
Constitutionalism, 61, 85
The conundrum of legislation morality, 77–78
Covenantal culture
   empowerment, 55
   healthy organization, 56
   integrative approach, 58–59
   organizational culture, 56
   Postmodernism, 56–57
   spirituality in the workplace, 58
Covenant and interpersonal relationships
   biblical idea of, 17
   boundaries, 21–22
   empowerment and collaboration, 20–21

Covenant and interpersonal relationships (*continued*)
- husbands and wives, 24–26
- imagine your friends, 22–24
- mutual accountability, 20
- mutual appreciation, 19–20
- mutual empowerment, 19–20
- parents and children, 24–26
- in spirit and in truth, 18–19
- theology of covenant, 18

Covenant-keeping, 18, 21, 27, 28, 53
Creation and redemption, 86–88
Creation mandate, 86, 87
Culture and communication
- leaders and followers, 52–53
- vision-building, 53

Culture wars
- America's political system, 111
- Christian legalism, 96–98
- gospel and covenant *vs.* the isms, 107–109
- gospel implications, 101–106
- impacts of false gods, 106–107
- Marxism, 100–101
- over-reactions to over-reactions, 98–99
- Postmodernist, 99–100

D

Dark and dying world, 38
Deuteronomy, 68, 85
Diatheke, 88
Dominium, 74

F

FAIL
- authoritarian, 97–98
- fear-based, 97
- isolationist, 98
- legalistic, 98

G

Gender specificity, 102
God covenants, 65
God of the Bible, 4, 57, 97

God's character
- incredible patience, 63
- notion of justice, 67–68
- overview, 66–67
- worship and enthusiasm, 66

God's sovereignty, 10, 28, 63, 66, 70
Gospel, 3, 7, 8, 12, 21, 23, 27, 32, 33, 38, 41, 42, 46, 48, 49, 79, 80, 87, 95–98, 101–108, 117
Gospel and covenant *vs.* the isms, 107–109
Gospel implications
- family life, 102–104
- privilege and racism, 104–106
- sexual intimacy, 102–104
- sexual temptation, 104

H

Hebrew Bible, 67
Hesed, 18–19, 21, 51–55, 58, 59, 84, 88, 90–92
Holy Trinity, 7, 8, 17, 27, 63
Humility and self-awareness, 30
Husbands and wives, 24–26

I

Idols of leadership
- avoid vision-killers, 49
- goal, 50
- idolizing results, 50
- measurement, management, and manipulation, 49–50
- personality-driven leadership style, 42
- promotion fallacy, 48–49
- raging control/abdication, 48

Impacts of false gods, 106–107
Insecurity-exploitation pattern, 64
Institutes of the Christian Religion, 71
Intrapersonal realm
- addictions, 11
- adoption, 11
- Christian perfectionism and legalism, 13–15
- dehumanization, 11
- God's love and intimacy, 15
- healthy vulnerability, 12–13
- justification, 8–9
- propitiation, 7–8

rebels, orphans, and slaves, 3–7
reconciliation, 9–11
redemption, 9
self-sufficiency, 11

L

Leadership
  definition of, 42–43
  between god and man, 44–48
  idols of, 48–50
  vs. management, 43–44
  nature of empowerment, 45–46
Legislate morality, 77, 82
Living Word of God, 5, 108

M

Man and man
  constitutionalism, 85
  covenantal empowerment, 85
  creation and redemption, 86–88
  hesed, 84
  idea of covenant, 88–89
  mutual accountability, 85
  non-centralization, 85
  notion of covenant, 84
Marxism, 65, 67, 100–101
Medieval era, 73, 75
Mishpat, 67, 68
Modernism-Postmodernism matrix, 106
Mosaic covenant, 86, 87
Mosaic law, 8, 87, 103
Multi-faceted conundrum of sin, 72–73
Mutual accountability, 85
  active dialogue, 54
  big picture thinking, 54
  covenantal approach, 53
  performance management, 54–55

N

Nature of man
  historical developments, 73–75
  imago dei, 69
  inalienable rights, 69–71
  multi-faceted conundrum of sin, 71–73

Noahic covenant, 70, 86, 87
Noncentralization, 85
  boundaryless communication, 55
  vs. decentralization, 55

O

Organizational leadership, processes, structure, and culture (OLPSC)
  best practices, 59
  covenant an integrative approach, 58–59
  federalism, 52
  hesed, 51–52
  mutual accountability, 52
  noncentralization, 52
Orphanhood and idolizing the state, 114

P

Parents and children, 24–26
Peace-breaking, 20, 27–28
Peace-faking, 27–28
Peace-making, 27–28
Pride and insecurity, 7
Privilege and racism, 104–106
Protestant Reformers, 83
Public policy
  covenant and tools for sound policy, 117
  crony capitalism, 116
  definition, 111
  human frailty, 111
  orphanhood and idolizing the state, 114
  radical revolution, 117
  rebels and the power of elites, 111–114
  removal of poverty and injustice, 116
  rent seeking, 116
  separation of Church and State, 115
  slavery, 114–116
  structural injustice, 116

R

Rebels and the power of elites
  economic planning, 113–114
  expense of competition, 112–113
Redemption mandate, 86, 87

Relationship between god and man
  biblical perspectives, 81
  church and state must have separate
      functions, 80–81
  Church over the State, 79
  hair-trigger approach, 78
  historical evidence, 82–84
  Pharisees, 78
  point of agreement, 79
  prideful approach, 78

S

Scripture, 3, 4, 8. 10, 17, 18, 28, 29, 51,
    57, 61, 62, 66–69, 71, 80, 83, 86–88, 92,
    96–99, 102, 104, 112, 113
Selfless self-defense
  basic life, liberty, and property, 90
  covenantally-proscribed powers, 91
  fighting tyranny, 92
  historical evidence, 93

inalienable rights, 90
slaves to sin, 90
spirit of vengeance, 90
Shapat, 67
Sin and problem of selfish empowerment, 46
Sin-crime distinction, 73, 80, 115, 116

T

Ten Commandments, 69–71, 87
Theology of covenant, 18
Transcend, 57, 82, 89, 95

V

Vulnerability and intimacy in Christ
  adoption, 11
  justification, 8–9
  propitiation, 7–8
  reconciliation, 9–11
  redemption, 9